Do-It-Yourself Decorating

Step-by-Step
Bed and Bath Projects

Heather Luke

Meredith® Books
Des Moines, Iowa

Contents

Very easy

A little skill

Some experience

Before You Begin

Bedrooms and bathrooms are two rooms in the house where you can truly pamper yourself. The only really practical decorating considerations are the bedding, which should be easy to launder, and the fabrics, which should be the best you can afford. Make sure that fabrics for shower curtains, laundry bags, and covered storage boxes are waterproof.

The projects in this book use basic methods and stitches that can be adapted to any situation. You may assemble projects by hand or by machine. The fabrics used have timeless appeal and are readily available in most fabric stores.

This chapter introduces the basic ingredients needed to complete the projects—fabrics, lining, and trimmings—and includes hints on color and style. You also will find guidance on selecting the right combination of materials and equipment to complete the project.

Style and color

You can choose almost any fabric or style of furnishing to decorate a bedroom. Do you want to create an intimate, feminine boudoir or a casual country-style retreat? Or perhaps you prefer a more austere room with clean lines and light colors. Create the mood that suits you best through fabrics and decorative details.

ROMANTIC OR COUNTRY STYLE

▲▼ To create a romantic bedroom, choose cotton organdy, silk organza, muslin, or embroidered lawn, and use swaths of fabric generously. Full, gathered bed curtains create a feeling of protective enclosure. For a country look, use woolen tweeds, rough hand-loomed linens, and patchwork covers to complement rustic furnishings.

PURE WHITE

▲ Whites and creams are light and ethereal. A neutral scheme with subtle touches of natural color (provided here by the terra-cotta floor, color-stained wood, and simple bands of color on the bed curtains) creates a serene environment conducive to rest and meditation.

FRENCH STYLE

▲ Toile de Jouy is a traditional French printed cotton that is perfect for creating an elegant bedroom with a formal feeling. It is available at every price level. This fabric has the great advantage of providing pattern without introducing confusing or strong color combinations. The soft cotton falls and drapes well and is usually washable.

COLOR COMBINATIONS

▲ Although there are no hard and fast rules regarding color in the bedroom, you might want to avoid bright hues such as sharp yellow, turquoise, and lime green. Softer tones are usually more restful, and they're kinder to the complexion. If you want to use rich colors, such as reds, greens, and dark blues, choose a shade with softer undertones, such as mulberry-red rather than bright purple.

SMALL DETAILS

◀ Pay attention to the small accessories. Always display a vase of flowers for color and fragrance. Good lighting, a mirror, a chair, a place to drop your clothes, and somewhere to comb your hair are as important as the room's fabrics and soft furnishings.

CREAMY TONES

▲ In a nearly neutral room that combines taupe, oyster, sand, and cream, textures bring the scheme to life. Try incorporating a variety of contrasting textures, such as knitted fabrics, leather, suede, cashmere, velvets, brushed cottons, and silks. Their touchable quality adds to the room's cozy comfort.

Choosing fabrics

Will you really have sweeter dreams if you sleep on 310-count Egyptian cotton sheets? Well, maybe not. But buying the best bedding you can afford is a good investment because it will last for many years of use and laundering. Linen or a linen-and-cotton mix is the most luxurious, but good-quality soft cotton sheets are more readily available and equally serviceable.

LINEN

▲ From the earliest times, fine linen sheets have been prized possessions. Linen fiber is obtained from the flax plant, grown mostly in northern Europe. Time-consuming to produce, and therefore relatively expensive, linen has no equal when it comes to bedding. Soft, strong, and very absorbent, linen can be washed at high temperatures and will resist years of wear.

COTTON

▲ Cotton is second only to linen for bedding and is available in every type of weave imaginable: waffle, twill, brushed, combed, satin, knitted, printed with floral or abstract designs, and woven into stripes and checks. Like linen, cotton is robust, absorbs moisture, and can withstand a lifetime of washing at very high temperatures. It's less expensive than linen; a fifty/fifty cotton/linen mix offers some of the luxury of linen at a lower cost.

PRINTS AND WEAVES

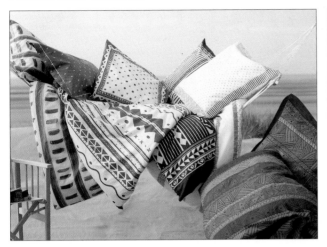

▲ Although it's a matter of personal taste, you may find that bold, multicolored printed bedding quickly becomes tiresome. Fine stripes and checks in soft, pastel shades are easier on the eye and combine well with florals and solid white. Avoid textured fabric for sheeting because the rough surface may be uncomfortable to lie on. Instead, use it to make decorative cushions.

BUYING WIDE-WIDTH FABRIC

▲ The normal width for furnishing fabric is 50 to 60 inches. Because almost all bedding is wider than this, it is helpful to buy fabric in a wider width. There are specialist mail order companies that supply fabric in 72- to 130-inch widths. Use this fabric for the top of a comforter or a duvet cover so you don't have to piece fabrics. Or use ready-made queen-size sheets to make a double-bed size duvet.

POLYESTER/COTTON

◄ The advantages of polyester/cotton fabric are low cost and easy care. Poly/cotton sheeting doesn't last as long as 100-percent cotton or linen, and its colors will fade with laundering. Also, it doesn't absorb moisture as well. If you plan to make your own sheets, be sure to buy the best fabric you can afford.

Using patterned fabric

Patterned fabric for the bedroom ranges from florals to plaids to whimsical prints with a lighthearted feeling. Don't be afraid to mix plaids and prints, either. As long as they're unified by a common color scheme, the effect will be harmonious and pleasing.

PATTERN REPEATS

◄ Combine large- and small-scale florals with a solid color for a romantic-looking bedroom. Remember that if you choose a fabric with either a printed or woven design, you will need to take into account the repeat of the pattern. Choose a prominent part of the design—the top of a large leaf or the bottom of a basket, for example—and measure to the exact same spot on the next pattern up. This is your repeat. For each length (cut) of fabric, you will need to check how your repeat will fit, and cut up to the next repeat. If a given length is 84 inches and your pattern repeat is 26 inches, your cuts will include three complete patterns, plus a little more—78 inches for three repeats. Four repeats will bring the length to be cut to 104 inches. Save the remnants to make pillow ruffles, table scarves, and trimmings.

THE CONTRASTS

▲ Contrasting textures and patterns create tactile and visual interest. For example, combine linen sheets with printed cotton pillow covers. Add a cotton duvet that's plaid on top and patterned on the opposite side and a throw made from the softest flannel. Hang silk draperies lined with muslin at the window, and you've created a happy mix of luxurious and inexpensive fabrics. Alternatively, use ordinary black-and-white mattress ticking to skirt a bed dressed with crisp white sheets and pillows. Cover them with sprigged cotton lined with muslin, and toss on a pair of silk cushions in strong colors to provide the spark.

USING WHITES

◀ It's hard to match the pure, unadulterated simplicity of white in any of its manifestations—pure white, oyster, vanilla, unbleached linen, or parchment. A white theme looks as good against a background of rich red or green as it does against the palest yellow or pink. White is crisp and fresh in summer and provides a foil for heavy winter bedding. If you have only one set of bedding, make it white.

THE SEASONS

◀ Change your bedroom with the seasons. Make one set of bed curtains for winter and one for summer, and stitch up reversible comforters and bedcovers. Toile de Jouy and tartan are perfect companions—the one crisp and fresh for summer, the other warm and comforting in winter. Or pair primitive sprigged cottons with shot taffetas, country checks with rural tweeds, or wool with muslin.

PREPARATION

Before you cut any fabric, thoroughly check it for flaws. Faults in the weave do occur in weaving and printing, and the design size can vary by a few inches from bolt to bolt. Carefully work out the pattern repeat and try to hide any small flaws in hems and headings. Cut along the grain for a plain fabric and to a pattern line for a print. Technically, the pattern should be printed exactly on the grain, but in reality, this will only happen with the most expensive cloth. Always check laundering compatibility when using different fabrics together.

Fillers and trimmings

The way you line, support, and insulate the soft furnishings in your bedroom and bathroom is as varied as the choice of the furnishing fabrics. What you use depends on whether you prefer synthetic or natural fillers and whether the curtains are to be used in summer or winter. If you suffer from allergies, you'll want to choose synthetic materials instead of down.

LINING AND INTERLINING

▲ A lining fabric adds weight and bulk and protects the main fabric from dust and sunlight. It also provides a neat backing for your work. Buy 100-percent cotton curtain lining or plain poplin if you want a color to match the main fabric. Use curtain lining for bed skirts and behind headboards and canopies. Sandwiched between the main fabric and the lining, an interlining is used to provide bulk to curtains. Most are 95-percent cotton and washable. The heaviest weight is called bump and the lightest is domette. Use them in place of polyester batting if you want to avoid synthetic fibers.

THREAD

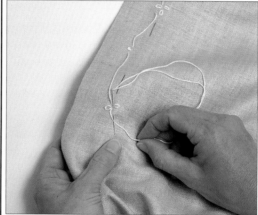

◄ Always match the washing requirements of the thread to the fabric. If you are using silk, buy silk thread. For cotton and linen, buy cotton thread. Use cotton thread for wool and a polyester/cotton mix for synthetic fibers. Use polyester thread for stretchy fabrics.

BATTING

◄ Very light and washable, polyester batting is used for quilted bedcovers, pillow covers, and headboards. It is available in several widths and weights— low-loft for appliqué and light quilting, medium-loft for normal quilting, and high-loft for bedcovers. Cotton batting isn't washable and comes as a fluffy mixture held between thin layers of cotton or paper. Use this only for fine work on silk, cotton, and linen.

PILLOWS AND CUSHIONS

▲ Top-quality pillows are filled with down from the eider duck. They are very soft, can be squashed and plumped easily, and are also the most expensive. A feather/down mix is more economical, and the least expensive feather pillows are filled with coarse chicken feathers. Buy the highest down-to-feather ratio you can afford. Allergy sufferers should choose synthetic-fiber-filled pillows.

TRIMMINGS

◄ Whether decorative, functional, or both, buttons and ribbons must have the same laundering requirements as the fabric. Most ribbons are pre-shrunk when you buy them, but as an extra precaution, wash them before stitching. Attach buttons with buttonhole thread, strengthened with a dab of clear nail varnish.

DUVETS

◄ Duvets fall into the same categories as pillows. Each duvet has a fill power that denotes a level of warmth: the higher the fill power, the warmer the duvet. Many people prefer a fiber filling, which can be laundered in a washing machine and is kinder to allergy sufferers. During the warmer months, hang duvets out to air whenever possible, and clean them every couple of years.

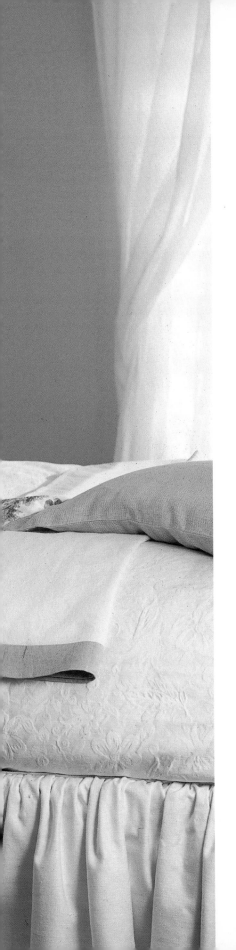

Bedroom Basics

Although you can find perfectly beautiful bedding in specialty and department stores, making your own allows you to choose from a wider array of fabrics—and you can dress your bed in a style that's uniquely yours. Bed skirts are always much fuller and of a better weight if you make your own. It's also easy to stitch up your own bolsters and cushions, and you can choose the sizes, trims, and fabrics best suited to your decorating style.

If you feel daunted by the thought of finishing a whole bed, why not buy one set of pillow shams and make another? Or decorate purchased linen with appliqué and decorative stitches. This way you will be creating your own personalized look without having to invest quite as much time.

This chapter contains

Decorative bed linen

If you haven't the time to make your own bedding (or if you can't find wide-width fabric in your area), decorate ready-made items instead. For the best results, choose sheets of the highest-quality 100-percent cotton, 100-percent linen, or a 50/50 linen/cotton mix. Appliqué, cross-stitch, and embroidery are time-honored techniques for embellishing bed linens and giving them an heirloom quality. (Embroidered pillowcases make wonderful keepsake gifts, too.) Ribbons also are ideal for decoration. Choose pillow shams that offer a generous stitching area and select sheets with a good turn-back hem at the top.

MATERIALS:
Pillow sham, sheet, embroidery thread, ribbon, matching sewing thread

FABRIC:
Ribbon-trimmed pillow sham: Pillow sham, enough 1-inch-wide ribbon to go twice around the outer edge of the pillow sham, plus 10 inches for each corner bow
Embroidered sheet: Sheet, enough 1-inch-wide ribbon to go across the top of the sheet, embroidery thread

RIBBON-TRIMMED PILLOW SHAM

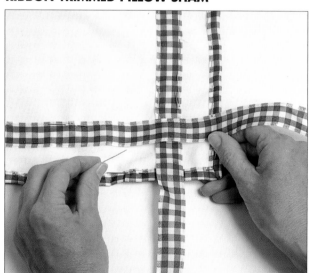

1 On the pillow sham, fold ribbon in half lengthwise over the outer edge of the sham, mitering the corners and pinning the ribbon in place as you go. Pin another row of ribbon just outside the inner line of stitching on the pillow sham, leaving tails for corner bows.

2 Baste along the center of each ribbon trim, then machine-stitch ⅛ inch from the outer edges of the ribbon. Always stitch in the same direction around the pillow to keep the ribbon from puckering. Remove basting stitches. Tie ribbon bows at each corner and tack in place.

EMBROIDERED SHEET

To make the embroidery stitches appear the same on the back side as on the front, always carry the threaded needle between the two fabric layers. Use straight pins or a water-soluble marker to mark the centers for French knots and crosses in a row 1 inch above the ribbon border.

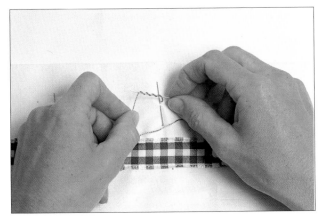

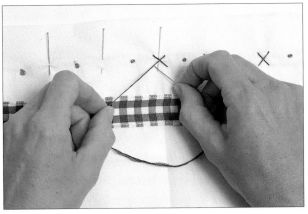

1 Stitch ribbon across the top of sheet (see Sham, Step 2). Using embroidery thread, work a French knot (page 84) on the top of the sheet. Push the needle through to the back; make another knot.

2 For cross-stitches (page 84), make the first stitch so it shows on the front and back of the sheet. Carry the needle between the fabric layers to the upper right corner of the cross; make second stitch.

WOOL-EMBROIDERED BLANKET

To spruce up the edge of a purchased blanket, add hand stitches using your own colored wool. Along the edge of the blanket just inside the stitching, make an inner row of French knots and cross-stitches to match the design embroidered on the sheet. Don't worry about making the stitches absolutely perfect—a little irregularity just adds to the handcrafted, homespun look.

Pillow covers

Pillow covers offer endless opportunities to add a splash of color or a change of style to any bed, and they can be easy and inexpensive to make. Try changing them with the seasons: Start with pretty covers of floribunda roses and fresh stripes paired with crisp white linens for the summer. At the onset of colder weather, swap them for covers of richly colored and textured wool, plaid, and velvet.

MATERIALS:

Any cotton or wool fabric—lightweight lawn for the summer and heavier fabric such as damask, velvet, or wool for the winter; matching sewing thread, seam binding for the ruffled cover

FABRIC:

For each pillow cover, 20×28 inches: Cut two 21¼×29¼-inch pieces of fabric. Your finished pillow cover should be ¾ inch wider and longer than the pillow for fitting ease.

For the tied cover only: One 8×41¼-inch piece of fabric for the flap, two 4×20-inch strips of fabric for ties

For the ruffled cover only: One 7×60-inch strip of fabric for the ruffle, one 1×41½-inch piece of seam binding

TIED COVER

1 Make up the ties, following the instructions on page 86. Place the pillow cover front and back together with the right sides facing. Using a ⅝-inch seam allowance, pin, baste, then stitch together, leaving one short side open. Trim the seams and snip across the corners. Turn the cover right side out and press.

2 Make a ½-inch hem on one long side of the flap piece. With the right sides facing, sew the short edges of the flap together. Trim, then press the seam open. With right sides facing, raw edges even, and matching the flap seam with the bottom pillow cover seam, pin the flap to the pillow cover.

3 Place one tie midway on each side, slipping the ties between the pillow cover and the flap, raw edges even. Stitch flap and ties to pillow cover. Turn right side out. Work a row of topstitching around the flap over the ties for extra strength. Slip pillow inside cover; tuck flap over pillow end, and hold it in place with a bow.

RUFFLED COVER

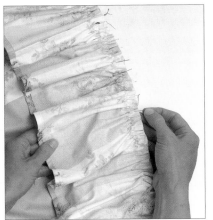

1 Using a French seam, join the short ends of the ruffle piece to make a circle. Stitch a ½-inch double hem along one long edge. Run a gathering thread ⅝ inch from the raw edge. Divide into four equal sections, tacking each division with a single stitch to mark it.

2 With right sides facing and using a ⅝-inch seam allowance, join the covers. Leave one short side open. Turn right side out and press. Divide the cover opening into four equal sections; tack each with a stitch. Pin the ruffle to the cover, right sides facing and matching tacks.

3 Pull up the gathers evenly in each section. Keep the raw edges even and pin each section at ⅝-inch intervals. Machine-stitch ⅝ inch from the raw edge, then trim the seam to ½ inch. Fold the binding tape over the seam and slip-stitch to the stitching line on both sides.

Bed bolsters

With their long, round shapes, bed bolsters offer an interesting visual contrast to the square and rectangular pillows piled luxuriously on the bed. They can also be entirely practical by comfortably supporting the small of your back as you read in bed. A bolster can be as simple as a "sausage" tied at both ends, or more elaborate, with buttons, piping, and tassels.

MATERIALS:
Fabric, matching sewing thread, piping, pillow form, ribbon for ties, cardboard for the bolster with buttoned ends, adhesive tape

FABRIC:
Piped bolster with ties, approximately 36 inches long and 10 inches in diameter: One piece of fabric 34½×37 inches, two 11¼-inch-diameter circles of fabric, four 20-inch lengths of ⅝-inch-wide ribbon for ties, and 2 yards of self-covered piping (see pages 88 and 89 for instructions)

Bolster with buttoned ends, approximately 36 inches long and 10 inches in diameter: One piece of fabric 34½×47 inches, four 20-inch lengths of ⅝-inch-wide ribbon for the ties, two 2-inch-diameter circles of cardboard, two 3½-inch circles of fabric, and 40 inches of narrow tape

Bolster with knotted ends: One 32½×72-inch piece of fabric, ribbon or fabric to make the ties (see page 86)

PIPED BOLSTER WITH TIES

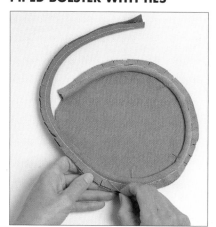

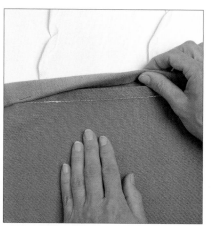

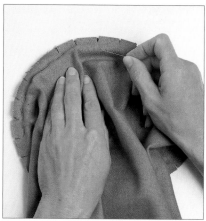

1 Snip into the piping seam allowance at ⅝-inch intervals. Pin the piping around the outer edge of one fabric circle, joining the piping ends. Baste and stitch the piping in place. Repeat with the other circle.

2 Fold the bolster fabric in half lengthwise with right sides facing. Using a 1⅝-inch seam allowance, stitch 8 inches at each end on the long edge. Stitch ties, equally spaced, on each side of the opening. Fold the seam allowance over twice. Stitch near the fold.

3 Pin the piped circles to the ends of the bolster with right sides facing. Baste, then stitch together. Trim the seam allowance, turn right side out, and press. Insert the pillow form and tie the closures.

BOLSTER WITH BUTTONED ENDS

KNOTTED END

To make a knotted bolster cover, stitch a single piece of fabric to make a tube. Trim the ends of the tube even, then insert the pillow form. Gather up each end and tie with ribbon or fabric ties.

1 To make the cover, follow Step 2 of the piped bolster on the previous page. Press under ⅝-inch double hems at each end of the tube. Sew a ½-inch-wide casing around the end of the tube, leaving a ¾-inch opening at each seam line. Using a bodkin or safety pin, thread narrow tape through each casing. Pull up tight, then knot the tape.

2 For each button, run a row of gathering stitches around the outer edge of each fabric circle. Center one cardboard circle on the wrong side of each fabric circle. Pull up the gathering threads and secure. Slip-stitch one button to each end of the bolster. Insert the pillow form, and tie the closures.

Throws

Cozy up your bedroom (or living room or sitting room) with a thick, soft throw. Tossed across an upholstered chair or the end of the bed, a throw introduces texture and color into your bedroom decorating scheme—and it serves the purely practical purpose of an extra blanket on a cold night! Indulge in an extravagant fabric such as chenille, soft wool plaid, or cashmere for snuggling. If your throw is strictly for show, consider shot taffeta, crunchy linens, or simple cotton checks. A handmade throw makes a wonderful holiday gift, too.

MATERIALS:

Reversible woven fabric with threads loose enough to pull away to make the fringe (for example, Scottish tartan, suiting tweed, heavy damask, rough woven cotton, linen, or wool in stripes or plaids, or heavyweight upholstery fabric), matching sewing thread, medium-weight cardstock for gauge

FABRIC:

Dress throw or single-bed cover: You will need 2¼ yards of 45-inch-wide fabric

Larger bed cover: You will need 5½ yards of 54-inch-wide fabric cut crosswise into two 2¾-yard pieces. Cut one piece in half lengthwise. Join the two pieces to each side of the wider piece with flat-fell seams.

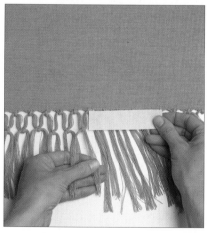

1 Pin the fabric to the worktable or weight it flat. Pin, then baste a line across the width of the fabric 6 inches from each end. Halfway across, make a cut from the raw edge to the basted line. Remove all the threads, one at a time, across one half width from the raw edge to the basted line. Repeat for the other half and again for the opposite end.

2 Divide the raveled edge of the fabric into ⅜- to ⅝-inch sections. Mark with small tacks or pins along the existing basted line. In each section there should be roughly the same number of threads. Take the threads from the first two sections and knot together against the fabric. Tie knots in this manner all the way across.

3 Before tying the second row of knots, make a 1¼×2⅜-inch gauge from cardstock. Leaving the first bunch of threads untied, tie the second and the third bunches together loosely. Hold the gauge between this knot and the knot resting against the fabric. Correct the distance, then secure the knot. Repeat across the width and on the opposite end.

4 Comb out the fringe, neatening the threads so that they are aligned. Place a straight edge on the fringe to hold it in place. Carefully trim away any uneven threads, using a sharp pair of scissors.

REVERSIBLE THROWS

Reversible throws can be made more substantial if you want to use them as bed covers. Choose two fabrics that are compatible for laundering and complementary in style and color. A richly colored wool plaid reversed with rough textured linen would be

a good summer/winter combination. Then fringe either both fabrics or just one. Throws also can be made with a plain bound edge, following the instructions on pages 38 and 39.

Gathered bed skirt

Bed skirts (attached to a plain, platform base) fit under the mattress and usually hang over three sides of the bed. Most skirts extend to the floor, but a shorter skirt may suit a low twin bed or a child's bed.

You can use almost any fabric for a bed skirt. A solid, dark-colored fabric can add visual weight to the bed, while delicate organdy will create an ethereal look. In either case, coordinate the skirt fabric with the coverlet or canopy for a unified effect.

MATERIALS:
Canvas or lining fabric for the platform base, any fabric for the edges and skirts, sewing thread, piping (optional)

FABRIC:
Platform base: Measure the width and length of the bed, and subtract 6 inches from each measurement. Cut and piece fabric to form a base to this size.
Edges: Cut four 4¾-inch-wide strips, cutting two the length of the bed plus 1½ inches (for ¾-inch seam allowances) and two the width of the bed plus 1½ inches.
Gathered skirt: Make as one piece or divide into three pieces to fit around corner posts. Measure the skirt depth, adding 4¾ inches to the hem and ¾ inch to the top and sides. Allow 2½ times around the bed for gathers.

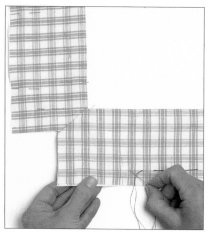

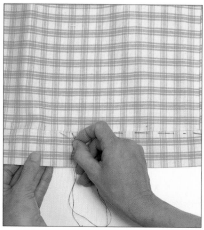

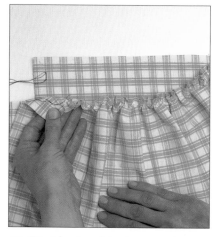

1 Press under ⅝ inch on one long (top) side of each edge piece. Pin, then topstitch each strip to the edges of the base, mitering the corners. Lay the base flat on the bed to check the fit. Cut to shape around the corners, adding a ¾-inch seam allowance. Divide the bottom and side edges into four sections; mark with single stitches of colored thread.

2 Whether you make the skirt as one long piece or in separate pieces for each of the three sides (the foot and both sides of the bed), hem the short sides of the skirt pieces. Pin, baste, then machine-stitch a double hem on the bottom skirt edges. Make another row of machine stitches ¼ inch from the bottom of the skirt.

3 Divide the skirt into twelve equal sections (or each side into four sections), and mark with colored thread. Make a gathering stitch between each thread ¾ inch from the top edge. Add piping around platform base, if desired (see pages 88 and 89). Pin skirt(s) to the sides of the base, matching colored threads. Pull the gathers and distribute them evenly.

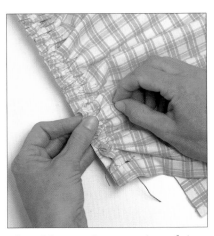

4 Pin the gathered skirt at ⅝-inch intervals along the length, leaving the pins in place to keep the gathers straight. Machine-stitch, using a ¾-inch seam allowance. Stitch again ⅛ inch towards the raw edge. Neaten the raw edge of the seam with an overlocker, zigzag stitches, or seam binding tape. Press, then stitch seam allowance toward platform base.

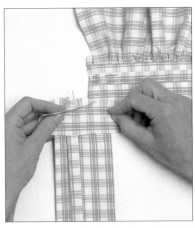

5 To neaten the top edge (head of the bed) turn under, then stitch the top edge of the base. For shaped corners, trim the edges with a fabric binding. Stitch ½-inch-wide fabric ties at each corner to tie around the bed legs to hold the skirt in place. Remove all tacking stitches, then press.

Straight and pleated bed skirt

A straight bed skirt with corner pleats creates a clean, tailored look. Worked up in cotton duck or canvas, the skirt suits a chic, contemporary room; in rich damask, it takes on an elegant air.

For a formal bedroom, the skirt should just skim the floor. On a more casual wooden or metal frame bed, you could use a slightly shorter skirt.

MATERIALS:

Canvas or lining fabric for the platform base, any medium-weight fabric heavy enough to fall along the length of the bed without sagging, lining fabric, piping, matching sewing thread

FABRICS

Platform base, edges, and piping: Measure the bed following the instructions given on pages 78 and 79.

Platform skirt: For these instructions the skirt will be made up in one length, falling from the sides and foot of the bed. Measure the required depth of the skirt and add 2½ inches for the hem and ¾ inch for the top seam. Allow about two widths of fabric for each side and one or two for the foot.

Platform corner flaps: The pleats at each corner are neater if made as separate flaps. You will need one 18- to 20-inch-wide flap for each corner. Cut the flaps from the main fabric, allowing about two widths for the four flaps.

Lining: Cut lining fabric to fit the skirt and flaps.

1 Assemble the platform base and edges following the instructions on page 24. Pin the piping around the edge of the platform, snipping into the seam allowance to ease around the corners. Baste and stitch in place before removing the pins.

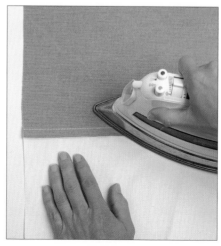

2 To line the skirt and flaps, pin the lining to the fabric along the lower edge with the right sides facing. Machine-stitch, using a ⅝-inch seam allowance. Open out each piece, and press the seams towards the lining. Turn under the sides of the fabric (but not the lining) ¾ inch, press, and baste.

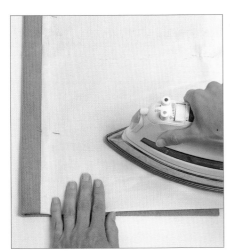

3 Fold the lining to the back, leaving 1½ inches of the main fabric showing along the hemline. Baste along the hem 1¼ inches from the folded edge. Trim ⅜ inch of the lining away at the sides. Fold under ⅝ inch and pin so that ¼ inch of the main fabric shows. Pin along the top edges. Trim away the excess lining. Slip-stitch all sides to close.

4 Pin, baste, and stitch the skirt securely to the edge of the platform base. Pin the flaps around each corner. Snip the seam allowance to ease. Baste and stitch close to the piping line. Stitch again all the way around, just inside the last seam line. Trim the raw edges by overlocking, pinking, or with seam binding. Remove the basting and press.

PLEATED SKIRT

For a pleated skirt, decide how many pleats you would like along each side, allowing approximately 12 inches of extra fabric for each. Make up each skirt in the same way as for the straight bed skirt. Mark the pleat positions on the platform side pieces before pinning the skirt in position, pleating the fabric as you go. Baste, then machine stitch the skirt onto the base. Trim the seam and press.

Pin-tucked cloth

Dressmaker details add panache to the simplest accessories. Pin-tucking takes some time and patience, but the technique is easy, and a small tablecloth offers a good introduction. Once you master the procedure, apply it to pillow shams and bed curtains, too.

The square cloth shown here nicely covers a display table, side table, or dressing table. Be sure to use washable fabric, or cover the table top with glass to protect the cloth if it's not easy to launder.

MATERIALS:
A plain, tightly woven cotton, such as lawn or organdy, silk taffeta, or a finely woven linen, matching thread, straight-edge ruler, water-soluble marking pen, pins, embroidery thread for decoration

FABRIC:
To make a 45×45-inch pin-tucked tablecloth, you will need a piece of fabric that measures 48×48 inches. Make sure you cut the fabric exactly following the grain.

1 Place the fabric flat on your worktable. Using a straight-edge ruler and straight pins or a water-soluble marking pen, mark the hem and five pin-tuck positions along one edge of the fabric. Allow 3 inches for the hem, $1\frac{5}{8}$ inches for each tuck, and $1\frac{1}{4}$ inches for the gaps between the tucks.

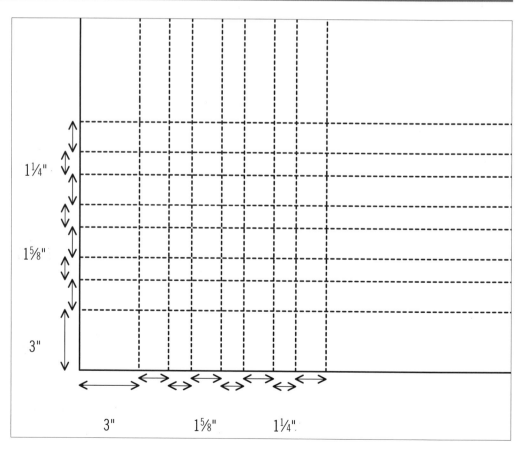

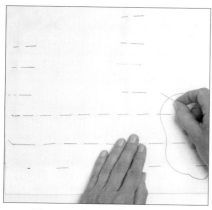

2 Baste along the marked lines, removing the pins as you go. Use a ruler to double-check the measurements from the hem up, as you work across the row. Turn under a 1½-inch double-folded hem. Baste, then machine-stitch close to the fold.

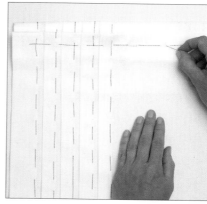

3 Working from the back, pin the top two rows of basting together. Finger-press. Pin the next six rows of basting in the same way to make a total of four tucks. Stitch just outside the basting lines to avoid catching the basting threads. Make tucks on the opposite side in the same way.

4 Repeat for the two remaining sides, stitching through the tucks on each finished side. Pull out the basting threads, and press carefully, keeping the pin-tucks straight. If you wish, weave contrasting embroidery thread through the top stitching line at even intervals.

Lampshades

Make quick slipover dresses for lampshades to update an old shade or change it to suit a new color scheme. Heavy paper shades or simple fabric-covered frames make the best bases for fabric slipcovers.

You only need a little bit of lightweight fabric to make the shade—a scrap from another project will do. Or treat yourself to an extra-special piece of fabric that might be too extravagant for larger jobs.

MATERIALS:
Lightweight sheer fabrics

FABRIC:
Gathered shade: Cut a fabric rectangle measuring twice the bottom circumference of your shade by the side measurement plus 5½ inches. You also need ½-inch-wide tape equal to the shade's top circumference plus 1 inch.
Tied shade: Draw a rectangle measuring half the bottom circumference by the side measurement plus 2⅜ inches. Mark and center the measurement for half of the top circumference of the shade on the top long edge of the rectangle. Redraw sides, joining ends of the bottom edge to the new top ends. Cut two shapes from fabric. You also need two 1¼-yard lengths of 1⅝-inch-wide fabric for ties.

GATHERED SHADE COVER

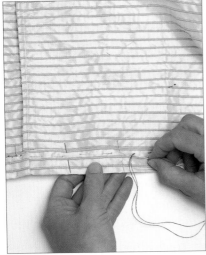

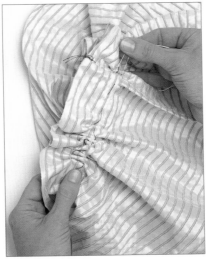

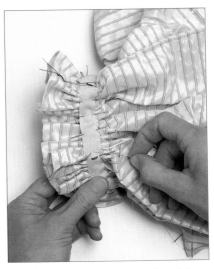

1 Join the short sides of the fabric to make a circle, using a French seam (make the seam as narrow as you can). Turn a 1¼-inch double hem to the wrong side along the bottom edge. Press, then baste in place. Slip-stitch through the fold line.

2 At the top edge, turn under 1⅝ inches and press. Run gathering threads 1¼ inches and 1½ inches from the folded edge. Fold the cover in half crosswise, then in half again, and tack each section to mark it. Loosely pull up the gathers.

3 Join the short tape ends with a ½-inch seam. Divide the tape circle into four sections, and mark them. Working on the wrong side, pin the tape over the gathers. Pull up gathers, matching tacks. Stitch around the top and bottom of the tape. Press; drop over the shade.

TIED SHADE COVER

1 To neaten the sides and bottom edge, press, baste, and stitch a ⅜-inch double hem along each edge on both fabric pieces. Trim away the excess fabric at the corners.

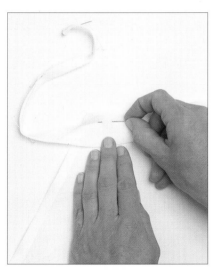

2 Prepare the two folded ties (see page 86). Unpin the center section of each tie; pin to the top edge of each fabric piece, matching centers. Stitch with a ⅜-inch seam.

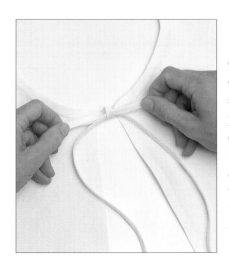

3 Fold over the tie to enclose the raw edges. Pin, then slip-stitch in place. Stitch the ends closed. Repeat for the other tie. Press. Tie the two bows, then slip the cover over the shade.

Quilts and Covers

The bed cover establishes the mood and style of the bedroom, but that doesn't mean that once you make your choice, you have to live with the same look forever. A reversible comforter lets you change the emphasis of a color scheme with a simple flip of the covers. You also can make duvet covers in different fabrics to change the room's look with the seasons.

An extra comforter or quilt can be folded neatly (or tossed casually) at the end of the bed, serving both a decorative and a practical function. The fabric you choose can play off the room's scheme with pattern or color that contrasts with the main spread. And on cold winter nights, you won't have to get out of bed to get extra covers.

Duvet cover

A duvet cover is an easy project for beginners, and it's among the most rewarding in terms of the impact it will have on your room. (Make pillow covers using the same techniques.) Choose feminine florals, sporty stripes, or crisp white cotton, depending on the look you want to create. If you like a change now and then, use contrasting fabrics for the front and back of the duvet and pillows.

MATERIALS:

Washable, easy-care cotton or linen, buttons, sewing thread, buttonhole thread

FABRIC:

Basic cover: Buy two sheets or wide-width sheeting fabric in cotton or linen. Wash and dry the sheets or fabric. Measure your duvet, adding 1 inch all around for seams and easement. Cut a front and a back. For a double cover, join the fabric with French seams.

Basic pillow cover: Measure your pillow and add 1¼ inches for the top and side seams and 5 inches for the bottom. Cut a front and a back.

Buttoned duvet cover and pillow: Cut front and back pieces as above, adding 15 inches extra to the duvet bottom edge. You also need six to 10 buttons for the duvet cover, three buttons for each pillow, and buttonhole thread.

Tied duvet cover and pillow: Cut the front and back pieces as above, two 9½×52-inch strips for plackets, 1⅝-inch-wide strips of fabric long enough to go around the cover for piping, 12 to 20 fabric strips measuring 1⅝×18 inches for duvet cover ties, and six 1⅝×18-inch fabric strips for pillow ties.

BUTTONED DUVET COVER AND PILLOW

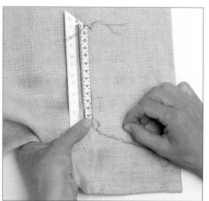

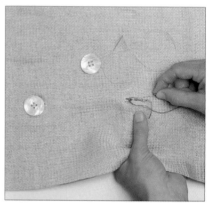

1 Place the two duvet cover pieces together with the right sides facing. Pin and baste 1 inch around the sides and the top. Machine-stitch, using a ⅝-inch seam allowance. Stitch again just outside the seam line (toward the raw edge). Trim the corners.

2 On the bottom edge, press 9½ inches to the wrong side, then fold 5½ inches to the inside, making a double hem. Pin, baste, and machine-stitch ¼ inch from the fold line and again ½ inch from the stitching line. Turn right side out and press.

3 Divide the hem width into 10- to 12-inch sections, tacking them to mark. Stitch a buttonhole at each spot on the top and sew buttons on the inside hem of the back. Dab the buttonhole thread with clear nail varnish. Make the pillow with a 2½-inch double hem.

TIED DUVET COVER AND PILLOW

1 Fold the piping material in half lengthwise (wrong sides facing) and press. Place the top cover right side up. Pin the piping to the cover, with the raw edge ½ inch from the cover edge. To miter the corners, ½ inch from the corner, fold the piping back on itself at a 45 degree angle and pin.

2 Baste and stitch ⅝ inch from the outside edge. With right sides facing, pin the duvet front to the back. Stitch inside the piping stitching line around the top and sides and 8 inches at each end on the bottom side. Trim the seams. Divide the opening into 10- to 12-inch sections. Stitch one tie in each.

3 Pin one placket strip to each side of the opening, right sides facing and raw edges even. Stitch just inside the piping seam line. Fold the remaining placket edges and ends under three times. Pin and slip-stitch the inner fold to the seam line. Turn duvet right side out. Press. Make pillow with a 2½-inch double hem.

Patchwork-lined bed cover

A patchwork lining for a bed cover is a great way to use up all of those scraps and remnants left over from previous projects. If your scrap bag doesn't offer enough materials, watch for sales in fabric shops, or scout yard sales for vintage fabrics.

Before beginning, launder the fabrics to make sure they are compatible. Almost any combination of prints will work, from solid colors mixed with checks and stripes to a multitude of florals. When assembling the patches, piece them randomly for a crazy-quilt effect, use same-size blocks for a simple grid, or select your favorite patchwork-quilt pattern.

MATERIALS:

Washable, easy-care cottons of about the same weight, piping cord, matching sewing thread

FABRIC:

Cover top, about 100×100 inches: 6 yards of 54-inch-wide fabric. Cut the yardage in half crosswise to make two 3-yard lengths. Cut one of the 3-yard lengths in half lengthwise, then join these smaller pieces to each side of the whole width.

Interlining: One piece of thin interlining the same size and assembled in the same way as the cover top

Patchwork lining: 441 squares, measuring 6×6 inches, or 100 squares, measuring 11×11 inches

Piping and finishing: 1¼ yards of main fabric for piping, 11½ yards of piping cord (Make the piping following the instructions on page 88.)

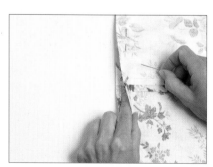

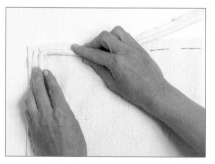

1 Stitch two patchwork squares together along one side, using a ⅝-inch flat seam. Snip away the corner at a 45-degree angle. Press the seam open. Continue joining squares in this manner, making 21 rows of 21 small squares or 10 rows of 10 large squares. Join the rows together, pressing the seams open.

2 Spread the top fabric wrong side up, and cut it to measure 102×102 inches. Place the interlining over the top, matching the seams. Lockstitch with seams matching. Trim the interlining sides to match the top fabric. Baste the two layers together ⅝ inch from the edges.

3 Turn the layers over so the top fabric is faceup. Pin, baste, and stitch the piping around the edge of the top fabric (see page 89). Press the seam. If the fabric is bulky, cut back the inner seam to ½ inch. Use herringbone stitches to sew the seam to the interlining.

4 Turn the fabric layers over (the interlining will be faceup) and place the patchwork lining on top, matching its center to the center of the top fabric. Finger-press under ⅝ to ¾ inch of the patchwork lining, pinning the folded edge close to the piping. Slip-stitch into the piping stitching line. Tie the layers together at patchwork intersections to keep the layers from shifting.

Reversible bed cover

Change your bedroom for the seasons with a reversible bed cover. Choose a richly colored and textured weave for the winter side and a lighter, fresher fabric for the summer side. Tough upholstery fabrics in crunchy linen or soft woven wool can be surprisingly inexpensive and will make lovely bed covers. Have fun with your fabric combinations. Partner a pretty floral chintz with wool flannel. Try a duet of a simple cotton plaid and a country tweed. Or, use rough, unbleached linen with sumptuous velvet.

Even if nothing else in the room changes, your bed cover will enrich or lighten the whole room from season to season.

MATERIALS:
Fabrics for the top, bottom, and binding that have the same laundering requirements; interlining, matching sewing thread, buttons

FABRIC:
Cover top, 100×100 inches: 8½ yards of 45-inch-wide fabric cut into twenty-five 22×22-inch squares
Cover bottom: 5¾ yards of 54-inch-wide fabric, cut into two 2⅞-yard lengths. Cut one of these lengths in half lengthwise and join one half to each side of the full-width piece.
Interlining: 5¾ yards of 54-inch-wide interlining, assembled as for cover bottom
Finishing: To make 3-inch binding from 2 yards of 54-inch-wide fabric, cut nine 8-inch-wide pieces across the width, then join to make one long length, using flat seams. You'll also need 20 buttons ¾ inch in diameter.

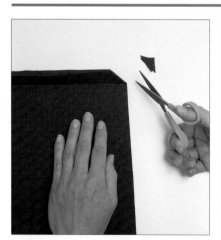

1 For the cover top, join two fabric squares together along one side with a 1-inch seam allowance. Press seam open. Snip away corners at a 45-degree angle. Join squares in this way, making five rows of five squares each.

2 Join two rows together, pinning seams exactly. Baste, keeping the pins in place at each seam junction. Stitch with a 1-inch seam allowance. Join the remaining rows in the same manner. Remove the basting threads and press.

3 Lay the interlining flat. Place the assembled cover top over this, right side up, leaving an equal border of interlining all around. Pin, then baste across the center and ¾ inch from the outside edges.

4 With the right sides facing, pin the binding to the edge of the cover top. Start at the top, about 12 inches from one corner. At the corner, let the binding extend beyond the edges and then fold it back on itself, leaving a folded flap. Baste as far as the seam allowance before the flap; fold the flap over and continue to pin along the next side, keeping the seam allowance exact.

5 Continue until you have pinned the border to all sides. Join the ends of the binding, using a flat seam. Machine-stitch 1 inch from the raw edges. At each corner, stitch up to the flap, backstitch, then lift the needle. Fold the flap over and turn the corner to continue stitching along the next side. Press the binding from the front, then miter the corners.

6 Turn the cover top over. Place the bottom lining fabric on top and baste it to the front and interlining inside the stitching line. These basting stitches will remain. Fold the binding over to the lining side to enclose the raw edges (the binding will be 3 inches wide). Fold under at the corners, mitering them opposite to those on the top. Press under the binding seam allowance so the fold aligns with the stitching line. Slip-stitch in place and press. Stitch buttons at each corner and intersection.

Quilted comforter

Quilting is an ancient and practical way to sandwich extra warmth between two layers of fabric. The results can be exquisite, and at its best, quilting combines art and craftsmanship.

If you don't have the time or expertise to create a quilted masterpiece, you can still enjoy the warmth of your own comforter. A simple machine-stitched cover quilted in channels offers the puffy softness and cozy warmth of a quilt but requires very little time to stitch up. If you enjoy quilting by hand, this comforter makes a good wintertime project—you'll stay warm under the quilt while you work on it.

MATERIALS:

Any fabric can be used. However, if you want to machine-quilt the channels, choose a fine fabric. If you want to hand-quilt, select a fabric that isn't too heavy, or the stitching will become laborious and uncomfortable. You also will need piping cord and matching sewing thread.

FABRIC:

Cover, approximately 60×80 inches: two pieces of fabric measuring 62×82 inches, a medium-loft quilt batting, and 8½ yards of piping cord or ruffle

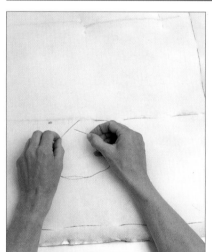

1 Place the top fabric flat on a working surface with the right side down. Lay the quilt batting on top. Pin and baste the batting to the top ¾ inch from the outer edges, then from the center to each edge. Machine-stitch around the outside edge ⅝ inch from the raw edges. Turn the piece over so the right side faces up.

2 With the raw edges aligned, pin and stitch the piping or ruffle to the top fabric, working over the outer line of stitching that joins the batting to the top. Clip and ease the piping at the corners as you work around the cover (see page 89).

3 Place the quilt bottom and top together, right sides facing. Pin them together along the top and sides. Baste, then stitch. Trim the corners and the batting, then turn the quilt right side out. Fold under the seam allowance on the bottom edges and close the opening with slip stitches.

4 To keep the fabric from slipping while you quilt, hand-baste the three layers together vertically, horizontally, and diagonally. Using a water-soluble marking pen, mark dots at 8½-inch intervals across the top edge of the quilt. Mark the same intervals across the center and the bottom edge. Using a yardstick, join the marks to create vertical lines. Hand-baste the full length of the cover ⅝ inch on each side of each line.

Roll up the cover and machine-stitch along each drawn line, always starting at the top edge and working down. Remove all basting stitches, then trim any loose ends.

HAND STITCHING

You may prefer to hand-stitch the quilting lines in patterns such as diamonds or interlocking circles. It doesn't really take that much longer to stitch, as long as you baste all of the lines firmly before stitching. Most designs are best set within a border, so mark a 6- to 8-inch-wide border around the outside of your quilt, then work a design of circles or squares within.

Tufted comforter

Start with a purchased duvet to make this cozy comforter. Simply sandwich it between the top and bottom covers and stitch the layers together. Embellish the stitches with handmade tufts of wool, cotton, or chenille for a finished look.

You can use almost any kind of fabric, even combining different fabrics for the bottom and top. (To make this project even easier, use purchased sheets for the covers.) Denim with a madras check or gingham and brushed cotton are appealing combinations for teenagers and children. Or for a sophisticated look, try linen with a ticking stripe or a velvet-and-wool mix.

MATERIALS:

Any fabric can be used, depending on how much you will be washing the cover; 60×86-inch single duvet, wool yarn or linen thread for the tufts, matching sewing thread, cardboard

FABRIC:

Top cover, for a 60×86-inch single duvet cover: Cut a 57×88-inch rectangle from fabric (the duvet cover is made narrower than the duvet to give the finished comforter extra fullness).
Bottom cover: Cut a 57×88-inch rectangle from fabric.
Filling: 60×86-inch single duvet
Tufts: Wool yarn or linen thread

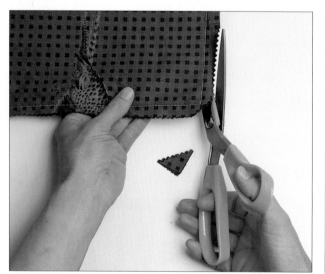

1 Place the top and bottom covers together with right sides facing. Baste around the sides and top. Stitch ¾-inch seams on the three basted sides, and then stitch 8 inches from each corner along the bottom edge. Trim the corners and the seam allowance. Turn right side out and press.

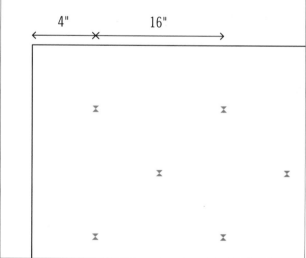

2 To mark the tuft positions, divide the cover into squares of 16 inches, leaving about 4 inches around the edges. (Whatever size cover you are making, try to keep the squares roughly this size.) Mark with pins and then tack with thread on both sides of the cover. Mark a spot for a tuft in the center of each square in the same manner.

3 To make the tufts, cut a piece of cardboard 1¼ inches wide. Cut a ⅜-wide strip out of the center of the cardboard as shown. Tightly and evenly wind a 50-inch length of yarn around the cardboard, centering it over the cutout. Cut a length of yarn 8 inches long, and tie it around the center of the tuft (working through the cutout). Pull tight and knot. Make 78.

4 Insert the duvet into the cover and shake it to distribute the duvet evenly. Pin at each corner. Slip-stitch the opening closed. Stitch one tuft on a tacked mark, pushing the needle all the way through the duvet and coming out on the tacked mark on the other side. Stitch a tuft to this side. Fasten securely and repeat with the remaining tufts.

Patchwork cover

Stitch this patchwork cover from your young child's favorite durable, washable fabrics, and it's likely to become an all-purpose blanket—spread on the floor for games, taken in the car on a long trip, and carried to a friend's house for a sleepover.

Sew together squares of favorite colors and mix in fabrics printed with popular storybook or cartoon characters. Or, choose fabrics featuring traditional timeless motifs, such as animals, alphabet letters, and numbers.

MATERIALS:

The top, back, and binding fabrics should all be of the same weight and fiber content. Colored denims, brushed cotton, twill, and wool flannel are all suitable. You also will need 24 buttons, matching sewing thread, wool yarn, and a tapestry needle.

FABRIC:

Single cover, 52½×93½ inches: From fabric A, cut six 13½×18½-inch rectangles and two 18½×44½-inch strips. From fabric B, cut seven 13½×18½-inch rectangles. From fabric C, cut two 16½×18½-inch rectangles.
Lining: Cut and piece a 55½×96½-inch rectangle.
Finishing: Use wool yarn for blanket stitching.

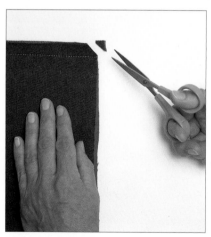

1 To join the fabric rectangles together, pin, then stitch using a ½-inch seam allowance. It is extremely important that the seams are all exactly the same size. Use a water-soluble marker to mark the seam line, or use the machine plate as your guide. Trim the end of each seam to a 45-degree angle and press the entire seam flat.

2 Sew the rectangles together in rows as shown in the diagram, opposite. Then sew the rows together to complete the top. Match the seams, then pin through the center of both. Pin all the seams and then in between. If there is any fullness, ease carefully. Baste, keeping the pins in place. Stitch, using ½-inch seam allowances.

3 Press all seam allowances open. Position the lining, wrong side up, on a flat surface. Place the pieced top, right side up and centered, on top of the lining. The pieced layer should measure 52½×93½ inches and the lining should be 1½ inches larger all around. Baste around the outer edges and across the center vertically and horizontally.

4 On each side of the pieced top, fold the excess lining in half to meet the raw edge. Fold again, covering the raw edge. Miter the corners and baste the hem in place. Stitch through all layers with blanket stitches, using wool yarn (see page 85).

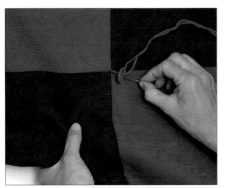

5 Using wool yarn, stitch a button to each side of the cover at the inside corners of the rectangles. Stitch through both layers twice and make a double knot to secure the buttons. Trim the wool yarn, leaving the short ends exposed. (Instead of wool yarn, you could use a narrow tape or ribbon.)

FABRIC PLACEMENT

Join the fabric pieces together following the diagram below.

A	B	A
B	A	B
	C	
A	B	A
	C	
B	A	B
A	B	A

Headboards and Canopies

Canopies and bed curtains, whether plain or fancy, add drama to the bed. Drape a single length of fabric from the supports, and you evoke nights on safari; hang swaths of muslin or toile de Jouy, and you create the sumptuous look of a royal bedchamber.

Filmy muslin and fine linen make wonderful summer curtains for the bed. Keep them for the winter, too, but add a second layer—of bright taffeta or wool plaid, for example—to make the bed look richer and feel warmer.

You don't have to have a four-poster bed to add a canopy. Poles hung from the ceiling can hold a length of fabric over the bed; molding attached to the wall serves as a crown from which curtains can hang.

Buttoned cover

Who would guess that a headboard hides inside this smart buttoned cover! Made from a purchased duvet and washable fabric, the design works perfectly in a child's room because the cover is squashy and comfortable, and it slips off for a quick machine-laundering.

You can cover almost any type of headboard with this treatment, including wood, metal, or fabric-covered. What counts is that the top is square so the padded cover will wrap neatly around the shape.

MATERIALS:

Any washable fabrics, such as cotton, denim, or brushed cotton for the main fabric and the lining; a single duvet, buttons, buttonhole thread, matching sewing thread, staple gun

FABRIC:

Headboard cover, 24×40 inches: One 47×56-inch rectangle each of main fabric and lining fabric, plus extra lining fabric to cover the headboard's edges; single duvet, eight buttons

Headboard cover, other sizes: To determine fabric size, add 7 inches to the width. Double the height and add 8 inches. The duvet should measure the width of the headboard and twice the height plus 8 inches.

Headboard: If you don't have a headboard, purchase plywood the width of the bed and 24 inches high. Cover it with lining fabric (see Step 1 below) or paint with matching paint.

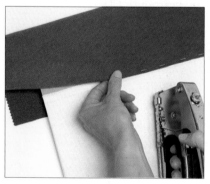

1 Cover the edges or sides of the headboard with lining fabric. To do this, fold strips of fabric in half lengthwise over the edges of the headboard; secure the edges with a staple gun or small tacks. Or paint the headboard to match the lining fabric so that when the sides are buttoned together, the bare wood will not show between the buttons.

2 Cut the main fabric and lining to the determined size and press. Pin the two fabrics together with right sides facing. Using a ⅝-inch seam allowance, baste, then stitch all around, leaving an opening about 24 inches long in the center of the bottom seam. Trim the seams, clip the corners, and press.

3 Cut the duvet to the width of the headboard and twice the height plus 8 inches. Finish the cut edges using an overlocker or a machine-zigzag stitch. Place the duvet on top of the fabric, centering it widthwise. Pin, then stitch along the top edge just inside the seam line and along the bottom edge ⅜ inch from the edge, leaving the opening free.

4 Turn right side out, press, then slip-stitch the opening closed. Pin and baste along the long edges ⅝ inch from each edge and then again 2¼ inches from each edge (use pins to hold back the duvet filler as shown above). Topstitch along the basting stitches, using buttonhole thread.

5 Fold the cover in half crosswise and pin the sides together. Mark positions for four buttons along each side. Make buttonholes on the front half. Stitch buttons to correspond on the lining side of the back half. Slip the cover over the headboard and button up the sides.

Slipcover headboard

Wooden and metal headboards look good, but they aren't particularly comfortable if you like to sit up in bed to enjoy Sunday breakfast or to read. A pile of pillows propped up against the back is one answer. Another is to make your own padded headboard using fiberboard, upholstery foam, batting, and pretty fabric as shown here.

MATERIALS:

Closely-woven, washable cotton, linen, silk, or wool; lining fabric, piping, ribbon ties, seam tape, fiberboard headboard, upholstery foam, batting and lining fabric to pad the headboard, matching sewing thread, paper for a pattern template, pencil, adhesive tape, staple gun

FABRIC:

Cover front, 24×40-inch headboard: One 28×44-inch piece of main fabric, piping to go up the sides and over the top of the cover
Cover back: One 28×46-inch piece of lining fabric, two 3⅛×25-inch strips of main fabric for the side lining borders, one 9×40-inch strip of main fabric for the top lining border
Side opening: Four 4×20-inch plackets, eight 12-inch lengths of ribbon, eight 20-inch lengths of white seam tape
Headboard covering: 28×44-inch piece of ¼-inch-thick foam, 28×44-inch piece of low-loft quilt batting, two 28x44-inch pieces of lining fabric

1 Lay the fiberboard headboard on top of the foam and cut around the outer edge. Place the foam on top of the headboard and temporarily hold with tape. Staple ⅛ inch from the edge all around the headboard. Lay the headboard, foam side down, on the batting. Cut around the outer edge. Repeat for the lining fabric, adding enough fabric to fold over to the back of the headboard. Lay the batting over the foam. Place the lining fabric on top. Pin both layers to the foam, then turn the headboard over. Fold the excess lining to the back of the headboard and staple. Cut lining to cover the back of the headboard. Fold under the raw edges and staple the lining in place.

2 Make paper patterns for the cover back and front, adding the widths of the board's top and side edges to the front pattern. Add seam allowances to both patterns. Cut a front from the main fabric and a back from the lining fabric. Also cut one top and two side lining border pieces from the main fabric. Baste, then stitch these pieces to the top and side edges of the back lining.

3 Lay the front cover fabric over the headboard. Make small darts at the top corners where the fabric extends over the edges of the board. Remove the cover from the headboard and pin, then machine-stitch piping around the sides and top of the front cover fabric, matching the raw edges.

4 With right sides facing, pin and baste the back cover to the front, leaving an opening on both sides the length of the side placket pieces. Machine-stitch along the basting line, following the edge of the cover and just inside the previous stitching line.

5 Pin the ribbon ties in pairs to each edge at the side openings against the piping. Repeat for the other side. Pin and stitch a placket strip to one of the four opening edges, with right sides together and covering the ribbon ties. Repeat for each placket. Press each strip in thirds, enclosing the raw edges within. Slip-stitch along the length. Attach ties along the bottom edge. Neaten the bottom edge and seams. Tie the cover onto the headboard.

Muslin curtains

Mosquito netting offers essential protection from insects in tropical countries. But the muslin fabric falls so gracefully that it's an excellent and inexpensive choice for purely decorative effects, too. Attach the fabric securely to the ceiling or wall with a small hook, and embellish the fabric, if you wish. Use ribbon roses and bows for a frilly look. Or use paint to stencil geometrics or even some summer wildlife on the muslin.

To soften a four-poster bed, you also can drape muslin over the frame and let it fall in soft "puddles" around the bed.

MATERIALS:
Muslin netting, fine cotton, organdy, organza, or gingham fabric for the curtain; ribbon, wire-edge ribbon, matching sewing thread, hook for wall or ceiling, cord or string, paper, pencil

FABRIC:
Rose-covered curtain: For a curtain that hangs 8 feet above the floor and drapes over a 60×80-inch bed, you will need six 3⅓-yard lengths of fabric for triple fullness, two 3½-yard lengths of ⅝- or ¾-inch-wide wire-edge ribbon for bows, and twelve 1⅔-yard lengths of 1½- to 2-inch-wide ribbon for roses.
Wavy-edge curtain: For the main fabric, measure from the floor to the canopy, across the bed, and back to the floor, and add 24 inches; for the border, piece 8-inch-wide strips to obtain this length.

MAKING ROSES

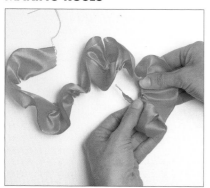  

1 Bunch the ends of the muslin lengths together and tie securely to a ceiling or wall hook. Drape the muslin around the bed so it falls in soft folds. To make the ribbon roses, run a gathering thread along one long edge of each (unwired) ribbon length. Pull up the thread, then coil the ribbon to form a rose.

2 Secure the gathering thread before stitching the ribbon layers together at the gathered end. Make a selection of different colors, sizes, and styles of roses. With looser gathering and winding, you'll make full roses; with tighter gathering and winding, you'll make smaller, tighter roses.

3 Stitch the roses together in groups, then stitch them to the muslin canopy, placing them randomly. Mix the colors and sizes of roses within each bunch. Tie a large bow from each length of the wire-edge ribbon. Stitch the bows to the top of the muslin over the bunched fabric, and add a few roses around the bows.

WAVY-EDGE BORDER

1 Accordion-fold the paper, then draw a wavy shape on the front fold. Cut along the drawn line and unfold the paper. This is the border pattern. Pin the long straight edge of the pattern to the straight edge of the border muslin, then cut along the wavy edge. Remove the pattern, then repin it further along the fabric edge. Keep attaching and cutting until the complete border length has been cut. Pin the right side of the border to the wrong side of the main curtain. Machine-stitch along the outside (straight) edge.

2 Turn the border to the right side of the main curtain, and press the seam so it makes a sharp edge. Pin the wavy edge of the border to the main curtain, and zigzag-stitch in place. Remove the pins and press. Drape the muslin curtain over the head of a four-poster bed to soften the lines.

Pin-tucked curtains

Often the most effective furnishings are those which are breathtaking in their simplicity. Curtains made from soft, filmy fabric make inexpensive, stylish bed curtains, even when they are as simple as panels with machine- or hand-stitched hems. For an elegant, understated look, add dressmaker detailing with a crown of tiny pin-tucks around the top. Satin ribbons, tied into neat bows, hold the panels aloft.

MATERIALS:

Sheer fabric, such as muslin, linen scrim, fine cotton lawn, organdy, or organza; matching sewing thread

FABRIC:

Curtains: Four lengths of fabric 52 inches wide by the length of the four-poster bed (or longer, if you want the panels to drape onto the floor), plus 6 inches for the hem

Curtain finishing: Four 1½×32-inch strips of fabric for the top binding, 26⅔ yards of ¼-inch-wide white satin ribbon for 48 ties, each 20 inches long

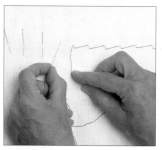

1 To mark the pin-tucks, measure, pin, and baste at ¾-inch intervals along the top edge and again 12 inches from the top. If you are making a V-shape with the pin-tucks, pin again 22 inches from the top. At regular intervals, measure back to the selvage to make sure the lines are straight.

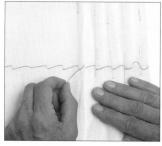

2 Leave 1½ inches at the edge, then pleat the next ¾ inch in half to make the first pin-tuck. Pin along the length for 12 inches. Pleat together every other ¾ inch all across the width, leaving 1½ inches at the other end. For the V-shaped design, follow the illustration and make 12- to 22-inch-long pleats across the fabric. Baste each pleat in place.

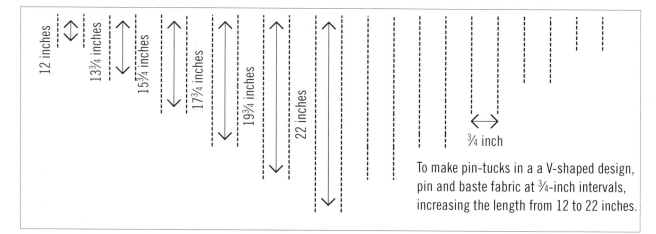

To make pin-tucks in a a V-shaped design, pin and baste fabric at ¾-inch intervals, increasing the length from 12 to 22 inches.

3 Machine-stitch the pin-tucks, using the machine plate as a guide and keeping the needle just inside the basted line. Remove the basting threads and press the pin-tucks in the same direction. Press a ¾-inch double hem on both long sides and a 3-inch double hem along the bottom of each curtain. Slip-stitch in place. Trim the top edge. With right sides facing, pin and baste binding to each top edge. Stitch the binding ½ inch from the edge.

4 Pin 12 pairs of ribbon ties, evenly spaced, across the wrong side of each curtain panel, raw edges even. Stitch the ties in place.

Fold the short edges of the binding to the inside, then fold the long edge of the binding over. Fold it in half again to enclose the raw edges, and slip-stitch the binding in place.

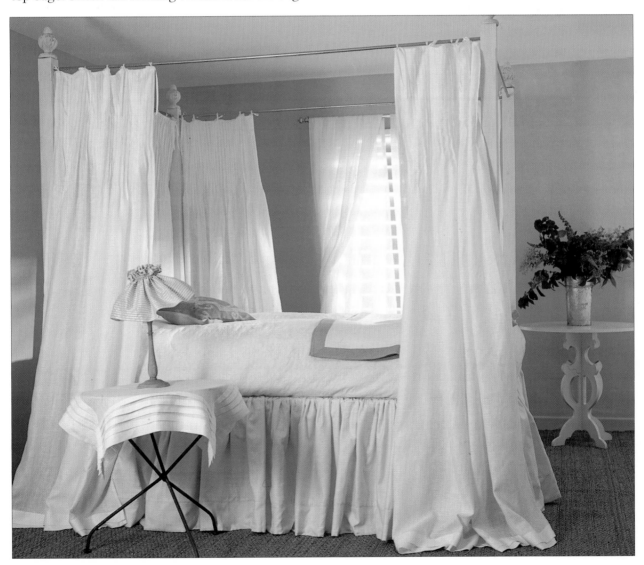

Tied bed curtains

Four-poster bed frames originally were designed to hold thick, heavy curtains. The curtains made the bed extra warm and cozy—a necessity, since few, if any, bedrooms were heated. Generally, tapestry hangings or heavy rugs were hung at each corner and pulled closed on all four sides.

Today, we curtain our beds for decorative purposes, rather than out of necessity. Even so, the panels should be full enough so they meet in the center when drawn. If they're made narrower, the end result may seem skimpy. If you like, add embroidery along the edges.

MATERIALS:
Lightweight or medium-weight fabric, matching sewing thread, embroidery thread

FABRIC:
Cut eight lengths of fabric 52 inches wide by the length from the top bar to the floor plus 6 inches for draping on the floor, 3 inches for the hem, and 6 inches for the self-ruffle heading. Also, cut 104 strips of fabric 4×18 inches (80 strips for the top ties and 24 strips for the side ties).

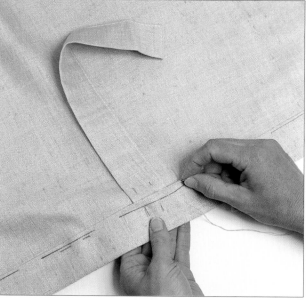

1 Place one curtain length onto a flat surface with the right side down. Press under 1½ inches twice along each side and at the bottom edge to the wrong side, mitering or folding at the corners. Along the heading, press under ½ inch, then 5½ inches. Make the ties (see page 86), folding in ½ inch on each long side, then folding in half to make the finished ties 1½ inches wide.

2 On one long side of each curtain panel, slip three ties inside the fold, spacing them 12 inches, 24 inches, and 36 inches from the top edge. Because the curtains will be tied together in pairs, half of the panels will need ties on the right side and half will need ties on the left side. Pin, baste, then stitch the side hems and ties in place.

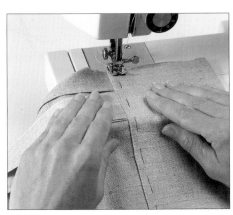

3 For each curtain, space five pairs of ties evenly across the heading, slipping about 2 inches of the ties' lower edges inside the heading. Pin, baste, then topstitch in place, catching the ties in the stitching.

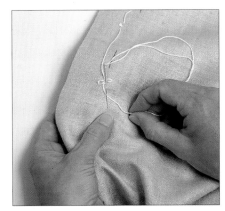

4 To finish the side seams and hem, stitch a simple embroidery design around all the edges in detached chain stitch, running stitch, and French knots. The stitches should be neat enough to be seen from both sides of the curtain.

Four-poster canopy

Because the posts on canopy beds originally were hidden by heavy curtains, the posts and headboard were usually plain. With the introduction of better heating methods, the curtains gradually became more decorative and less functional, so the posts and headboards were treated decoratively as well. (Eighteenth-century beds featured carved and fluted posts at the foot of the bed and plain ones at the head, where they would be hidden by fabric.) Today you can enjoy the four-poster unadorned, or add a simple, tailored canopy for a softening effect. This one, recalling Roman blinds, is easy to install and remove with ties.

MATERIALS:
Cotton or linen, matching sewing thread. (For a heavier fabric for the canopy and panels, choose a medium-weight fabric for the binding.)

FABRIC:
Small bed frame, 40×80 inches: For canopy panels, you will need two 1⅔-yard lengths and one 2¼-yard length of 40-inch-wide fabric. For binding, cut and piece bias strips of fabric to make 12 strips, each 2 inches wide and 32 inches longer than the side of the panel to which it will be attached. For eight pairs of ties, cut and piece bias strips to make 16 strips 2 inches wide and 16 inches long. *Large bed frame, 80×80 inches:* For canopy panels, you will need four 1⅔-yard lengths and two 2¼-yard lengths of 52-inch-wide fabric. For binding, cut and piece bias strips as directed above.

1 For the large bed only, cut one 2¼-yard panel in half lengthwise. Join one half to each side of the remaining 2¼-yard panel with French seams. Repeat this procedure with the 1⅔-yard panels to make two panels 60×102 inches. Trim the panels to the required width and length.

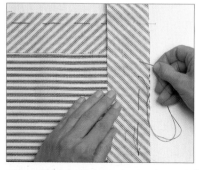

2 Place the canopy panel on a flat surface with the right side up. Along each side, pin a bias strip, right side down and raw edges aligned, centering the strip so 16 inches extend beyond each end. Baste and stitch ½ inch from the edge, starting and stopping ½ inch from the corner.

3 Fold under the raw edge of the binding ½ inch, then fold the binding over the seam allowance to the back of the panel. The fold line of the binding should align with the stitching line. Press the binding in place. Snip a ½-inch square out of each corner.

4 Fold and press the short end of each 16-inch extension under ½ inch. Then fold the raw edges to the center, and fold the extension in half again lengthwise to make ties ½ inch wide. Slip-stitch or machine-stitch the ties closed. Then slip-stitch or machine-stitch the binding along the canopy panel.

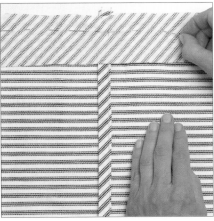

5 Repeat for the other two sections. If you wish to add extra ties at equal intervals on these panels, as shown below, make pairs of 16-inch-long ties. Pin them between the binding and the panel, raw edges aligned, before stitching the binding at the end of Step 2.

Over-bed canopy

Even if you don't have a four-poster bed, you can enjoy a canopy—just suspend a pair of poles from the ceiling, and drape a cloth over them. Screw heavy cup hooks into the ceiling joists (or install toggle bolts and hooks into a drywall ceiling). Then use S hooks to hold the chains that support the poles. Cover the chains with tubes of shirred fabric.

For the poles, you can use simple bamboo rods or purchased drapery poles. If you buy unfinished poles, you can paint or gild them to match the room's decor.

MATERIALS:
Double-sided cotton fabric, such as lawn or ticking, matching sewing thread

FABRIC:
4⅓ yards of 54-inch-wide fabric for the canopy, 1⅔ yards of 54-inch-wide fabric for the binding

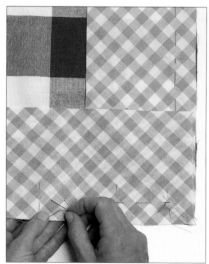

1 Cut the binding fabric on the bias into 3-inch-wide strips. Pin and stitch the strips of fabric together to make a 12-yard length of binding. Cut the remaining strips to make eight 2½×24-inch strips for the folded ties. Make up the ties following the instructions on page 86. With right sides facing, pin the binding fabric to the main fabric along all four sides.

2 To make the binding fit neatly around the corners, make a folded miter: Finger-press the excess corner binding material at a 45-degree angle; fold the flap onto the binding, and then back the other way to make sure it is even with the outer edge of the main fabric in both directions. Baste the binding to the fabric ¾ inch from the raw edges.

3 Following the basting line, machine-stitch the binding to the main fabric, stopping as you meet each corner flap and starting again on the other side. This will create a neat finish at the corners. Pin the ties in pairs, with raw edges together on the edge of the main fabric on each side, 60 inches from one end and 20 inches from the other end.

4 Press from the right side of the fabric. Fold the binding to the back, keeping an exact ¾-inch width all around the canopy. Fold the corner flaps to the right on the top and to the left at the back.

5 On the reverse side, fold under the binding fabric to make a ¾-inch-wide edging. Pin and baste the binding to the main fabric, then slip-stitch it to the machine-stitched line. Add extra ties to corners, if desired.

Scalloped corona

Corona curtains usually are held above the bed by a coronet-shaped circlet attached to the wall. The curtains drape to either side of the bed or sweep around the back and to the sides.

Lighter than a four-poster and less intrusive than an over-bed canopy, a corona can be hung with two or three layers of filmy fabric that can be allowed to hang in folds around the bed. The sides can be turned back and hand embroidered, adorned with ribbons or roses, or finished with a scalloped edge of creamy picot lace.

MATERIALS:

Sheer fabric, such as organdy, organza, muslin, fine cotton lawn, or fine linen; lining fabric, corona, curtain heading tape, picot lace, embroidery thread, matching sewing thread, medium-weight cardstock for the pattern template, pencil

FABRIC:

Two, three, or four 2¾-yard lengths of 54-inch-wide fabric (see Step 1 below), same amount of lining fabric, 9 yards of picot lace, 3¼ to 6¾ yards of ¾-inch-wide curtain heading tape

1 Attach the corona to the wall approximately 94 inches from the floor. If you have very high ceilings, you may want to fix the corona higher than this. For the curtain length, measure from the corona to the floor and allow for the drape of the curtain, adding 1⅝ inches for the heading. Two lengths will be needed if the drape is to hang to each side of the bed, three if the drape will hang around the back of a single bed, and four for a double bed. Join lengths of main fabric with flat seams. Repeat for the lining.

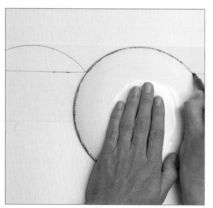

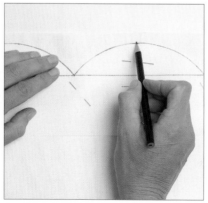

2 On a 2½×24-inch piece of medium-weight cardstock, draw a line 1¼ inches from one long edge. Position a saucer centrally on the line. Draw around the curve. Repeat along the cardstock. Cut out template.

3 Pin the template on one leading edge of the fabric and draw around the shapes. Start at the top, work down the edge and along the hem to the top of the opposite edge. Cut the fabric edge along the drawn line.

4 Pin, baste, and stitch the lace edge to the right side of the fabric, ½ inch from the cut edge. The lace should be pointing towards the center of the fabric so that when the curtain is turned the lace will face outwards.

5 With right sides facing, pin and baste the lining to the curtain 6 inches from the outer edge. Pin around the scallops and at the heading. Stitch together, following the shaped edge, just inside the previous stitching line (leave an opening for turning). Trim around the shaping and clip into each point. Remove the basting.

6 Turn the canopy right side out, and slip-stitch the opening closed. Press the scalloped edge, easing the fabric to make rounded shapes. Press the top edge 1⅛ inches to the outside. Pin the heading tape slightly more than ¾ inch from the folded edge. Baste and stitch the tape to the fabric. For added detail, work embroidery stitches along the scalloped edge.

Bathroom Accessories

Although the decorating focus in the bathroom is generally on the hard surfaces, you can add plenty of color and personality with "soft furnishings" such as the shower curtain, embellished towels, and even a laundry bag. The projects in this chapter are easy to make in an evening or in a few hours. Choose fabrics to match the color scheme of an adjoining bedroom. Or, if the bathroom is off the hall instead of a bedroom, choose colors and prints that coordinate with the overall style of your home.

Preshrunk cottons and linens are the most suitable fabrics. Watch for toweling remnants, tea towels, and napkins that can be used separately or joined in squares for linen bags and shower curtains.

For curtains around a shower or bath, look for fabric that can take steam without shrinking or staining. Line the curtain with a purchased waterproof curtain to protect your fabric.

Fabric-covered boxes neatly stacked in a corner or under an old-fashioned sink look pretty. They help keep the bathroom tidy, too, by storing toiletries, extra bath supplies, and any other items you might not want on display.

Shower curtains

It's easy to find ready-made shower curtains in any color or pattern, but to give your bathroom a distinctive look that reflects your style, the best solution is to make your own curtain. Because you'll be pairing (and protecting) it with a plastic liner, you can adapt items such as Battenberg or vintage '50s tablecloths, or decorate a house-painter's canvas dropcloth instead of buying fabric.

MATERIALS:

Washable outer fabric, waterproof liner fabric or clear or solid-color ready-made plastic shower curtain, metal pole to fit your shower area, ¾-inch-diameter eyelet set, matching sewing thread, ribbon for ties

FABRIC:

Curtain: For fabric (and liner) width, measure the pole length and multiply by 1¼, then add 3 inches (for 1½-inch-wide side seam allowances). For the length, measure the distance from the pole to the floor and add 4 inches each to the heading and the hem. You also will need 8 inches of ribbon for each eyelet.

Pole: Mount your metal pole at least 12 inches above the shower head. Plan on five to six shower-curtain rings per yard and the same number of eyelets as rings, plus three eyelets for each side.

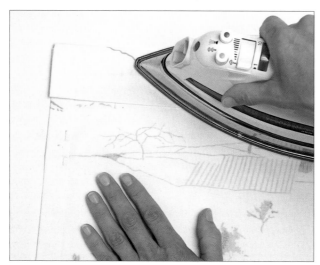

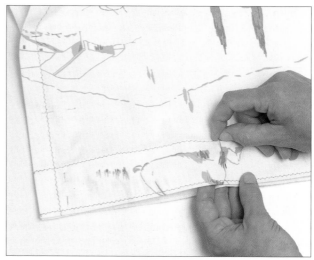

1 Press under ¾ inch twice on each long edge to the wrong side of the fabric. Pin, baste, and machine-stitch close to the inner folded edge. Press under 2 inches twice at the top and bottom of the fabric. Pin, baste, then machine-stitch close to the inner folded edge and again ½ inch from the outer edge. Press.

2 Place the waterproof liner or shower curtain flat on your work surface with the right side down. Place the fabric curtain on top with the right side up. Pin the layers together. They should be almost exactly the same size, but don't worry if they are not an exact fit. Simply ease the fullness of the fabric curtain evenly across the width.

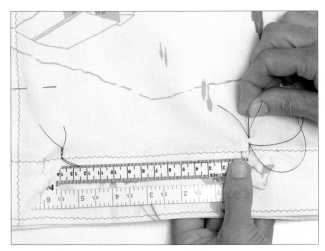

3 Mark the eyelet positions of both curtains with a stitch. If you're using liner fabric, make the first two 2 inches from each end and divide the remaining width into 8-inch gaps. Also mark three positions down each side with 16 inches between each. The last eyelet should be at least 40 inches from the hem. This lets you lift the waterproof liner inside the shower, leaving the fabric curtain outside.

4 Make the holes and punch the eyelets through, following the instructions with the eyelet kit. Using lengths of ribbon, tie the curtains together through each pair of holes and knot. Tie the ribbons to the curtain pole rings. If you find that you need to weight the liner a little, punch eyelets through this layer only, at the bottom corners.

PIN-TUCKED CURTAINS

A curtain in linen scrim will absorb up to 20 percent of its weight in water and can be machine washed and dried. This pin-tucked curtain is feminine and light. Or, use layers of muslin for a romantic effect.

Drawstring bags

Drawstring bags are easy to make, and they perform a myriad of functions in the home. Make oversized bags in white cotton, mattress ticking, or toweling for laundry bags. Use muslin for tiny lavender bags to hang in the wardrobe or a floral print filled with herbs for a cupboard or laundry room. Use any sturdy fabric to make bags for holding gym equipment, shoes, or toys.

A whole series of drawstring bags in different shapes, sizes, and fabrics are invaluable for traveling. Individual bags keep items in shape and protect everything from walking shoes, toiletries, and soft knitwear to a carefully rolled taffeta evening gown.

MATERIALS:
Choose a nonfraying fabric strong enough for the use of the bag, such as toweling or heavy cotton. You also will need a waterproof fabric (if the bag is intended to hold damp items), matching sewing thread, cotton cord, and bodkin or safety pin.

FABRIC:
Laundry bag, 20×28 inches: You will need one 22×63-inch piece of fabric, shower curtain lining fabric the same size as the main fabric (optional), and 3⅓ yards of ¼-inch-diameter cotton cord. If you are using lining, baste it to the main fabric, and use the two fabrics as one. *For other bags:* You will need a 6×16½-inch piece of fabric to make the lavender bag and a 14×36-inch piece of fabric to make a shoe bag.

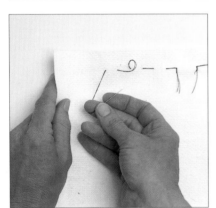

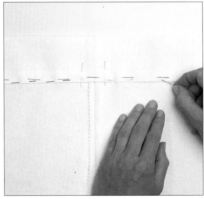

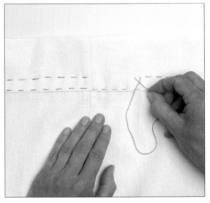

1 Fold the fabric in half crosswise with the right sides facing and the short ends matching. Using a ½-inch seam allowance, pin, baste, and machine-stitch each side, starting at the folded edge and stopping 7 inches from the top. Leave a ¾-inch gap, then stitch to the end.

2 Trim the seams with pinking shears, then press them flat. Turn over the top raw edge of the bag ½ inch, pin, and baste. Fold the top edge over again so that the fold ends just below the gaps in the side seams. Pin and baste.

3 To make a casing for the cord, hand- or machine-stitch all around the top of the bag ¼ inch from the folded edge. Make a second row of stitching ¾ inch above the first. Before threading the cord through the channel, decorate the bag with embroidery or appliqué shapes.

4 Press the bag. Attach a bodkin needle or a safety pin to the end of the cord. Thread the cord through the stitched casing, bringing the cord out on the same side you entered. Test for length, then cut the cord ends and knot them together. Repeat with a second cord on the opposite side.

5 Another way to make the channel is to add a strip of fabric to the outside of the bag. Cut a 1⅝-inch-wide strip of fabric to fit around the bag. Press under both long edges, then stitch the band to the finished bag. Start and finish on a side seam and leave the join open for inserting the cord.

Towels

It is possible to buy good cotton terry toweling, flat-weave linens, and cottons by the yard to make your own towels. You also can decorate plain ready-made towels. Simply bind the edges of the towels with fabric in a color that coordinates with your room decoration. Scraps of fabric can be employed for appliqué and bindings. And, if you enjoy hand embroidery, add initials or a decorative edge to the towels and face cloths.

MATERIALS:

Looped cotton, linen, or flat waffle-weave fabric, washable fabric with motif for appliqué, iron-on interfacing, ribbon or fabric scraps for binding, embroidery thread, matching sewing thread (Be sure to wash and dry all fabrics and ribbons before you begin to stitch.)

FABRIC:

Small towel, 20×28 inches: You will need a 22×40-inch piece of fabric.
Large towel, 20×35½ inches: You will need a 21×47¼-inch piece of fabric.
Note: Turn under a ½-inch seam allowance twice on each long edge and one short edge. Turn under ½ inch, then 5½ inches on the remaining short edge.

EMBROIDERED EDGINGS

1 To finish the edges of the towel without binding, turn under the seam allowance twice on all edges, using a deeper turn on one short edge. Pin and baste the seams. Remove the pins and press.

2 Using embroidery thread, work a row of large, evenly spaced running stitches close to the inner folded edge. Make another row just above the first, lining the stitches up with the gaps in the first.

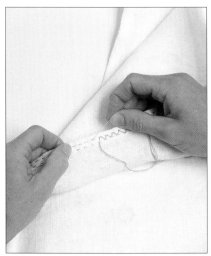

3 Using a contrasting colored thread, weave in and out of the two parallel rows of stitches, making a decorative zigzag stitch. The same thread can be used to embroider initials onto the towel.

BINDING

Ribbon or scraps of fabric can be used to bind the ends of the towel. The binding should look the same on both sides. For a 1⅝-inch binding, cut 5-inch-wide strips of fabric the width of the towel plus 1¼ inches for the ends. Press under ⅝ inch along each long edge and ⅝ inch at the ends. Fold the binding over the towel end, pin in place, and baste to hold both sides securely. Stitch close to the folded edge. You will need to make sure that the folded edges are exactly aligned so that as you stitch, you sew through both sides evenly.

BORDER EDGING

Use ribbons or fabric pieces to edge the end of the towel. If using fabric, cut strips the width of your towel plus 1¼ inches for the ends and 1 inch wider than you want the finished edging to be. Press under ½ inch along each long side and ⅝ inch at each end. Pin and baste to the towel. Stitch with tight zigzag stitches over the edge or straight-stitch just inside the folded edge. Ribbon can be pinned and basted on with the ends folded under and stitched in the same manner.

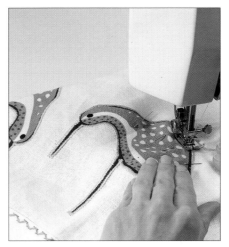

APPLIQUÉ

Appliqué is the needlework term for stitching one cutout piece of fabric onto another larger piece. The cutout might be a felt star cut freehand or a design from a printed fabric with a sufficiently simple outline that you can cut around easily and neatly. The cutout should be in proportion to the finished article. To prevent fraying, iron lightweight fusible interfacing onto the back of the appliqué fabric. Cut neatly around the shape. Pin and baste the shape onto the towel, using small stitches. Set the machine to a tight zigzag, and stitch around the outer edge of the shape. Always experiment on a spare piece of fabric before embarking on the real project. Remove the basting stitches and press.

Storage boxes

We all use storage boxes, but we often make do with old shoe boxes, shirt boxes, or other boxes originally intended for other uses. If your recycled boxes are sturdy, why not give them a facelift that reflects their new purpose? Covering boxes with fabric is easy to do, and you can make them even more useful by color-coding the contents— or choose fabrics printed with a design that reflects what's inside. For the office, covered boxes can store disks, videos, CDs, and all manner of papers, photographs, and birthday cards. Larger boxes are good for storing out-of-season clothes and linens. You can buy plain card boxes from department stores. They're inexpensive and sturdy enough to take a fabric covering.

MATERIALS:
Medium-weight, tightly woven cotton poplin or chintz. Patterned fabrics will hide any discrepancies if the box is bent and has less-than-perfect corners or joins. For the lining, use a nonfraying fabric, felt, paper-backed fabric, or paper. You'll also need tacky glue and a 1-inch-wide paintbrush.

FABRIC:
Main fabric: For a 3×6×12-inch shoe box, you will need one 4×37-inch piece of fabric for the box sides and one 11×17-inch piece for the outer lid.
Box lining: From lining fabric, cut one 6×12-inch inner base, one 6×12-inch inner lid, one 5½×11½-inch outer base, two 3×13-inch inner sides, and two 3×6-inch inner ends.

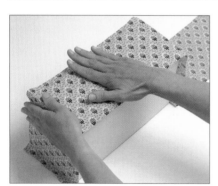

1 Add a little water to the glue to make it easier to use. Apply glue to one box end and one side. Place the long length of fabric on the table. Position the box end on the fabric, leaving ½ inch all around. Roll the box onto the glued sides. Press the fabric flat to remove any bubbles.

2 At the beginning corner, adhere the ½-inch overlap to the long side. Apply glue to the second end and side. Roll the box to attach the remaining fabric. To neaten the beginning (last) corner, trim fabric along the side of the box with scissors. The cut should be neat and the corner invisible.

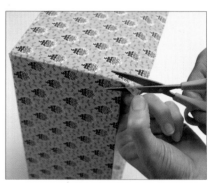

3 Apply glue ½ inch along the base of the box and press the fabric flap into the glue. At the top of the box, overlap the corners if the fabric is lightweight. For heavier fabric, cut away a triangle at each corner. Apply glue ½ inch inside the box, turn over the fabric flap, and press into glue.

4 Put glue on the box lid and center it on the lid fabric. Turn the lid over and smooth the fabric flat. Repeat to glue fabric to the lid ends. Pin the fabric tight to the corners. Fold, then trim back to ½ inch from the corner. Remove the pins and glue the flaps to the sides.

5 Place glue on the inner ends of the lid and along ½ inch on each side. Fold the fabric flap over, using scissors to push it into the corners. Repeat for the inner sides. At the corners, fold under the ½-inch flaps. Snip away the fold from the bottom of the lid, then fold one layer back inside the lid.

6 To line the box, apply glue to the long sides and along ½ inch on both short ends and the base. Press the side fabric inside, starting ¼ inch from the top so the lining extends onto the base. Score the creases. Adhere the ends, inner and outer bases, and the inner lid in place.

Tools and Techniques

This chapter covers the tools and techniques needed to create the bedroom and bathroom projects shown in this book.

Choosing the correct tool for the job is as important as selecting the right color or weight of fabric. You will find most of the tools used for these projects in a standard sewing kit. For the best results, buy the very best equipment you can afford—good cutting scissors, sharp needles and pins, and a strong measuring tape.

To help you make covers for different-size beds, duvets, and pillows, we've included a section on measuring. Here, you'll find the information you need to estimate the amount of fabric required for each of the projects in the book.

Proper care and regular cleaning will keep your bed linens and other soft furnishings looking their best. At the end of this chapter you will find information to help you protect your efforts.

Essential sewing kit

Good quality tools will last a long time and make it easier to achieve consistently good results, so buy the best you can afford. A sewing box with compartments will keep everything separate and easy to find.

MEASURING AND MARKING

Tape measure: This is a vital part of any sewing kit. Choose a tape measure made of nylon or some other material that will not stretch; the tape should have protective metal ends. Each side of the tape should start and finish at opposite ends so that you do not have to unwind the tape to find the starting point.

Steel tape: This is the most reliable tool for measuring items such as beds, windows, and curtains when working out quantities of material required.

Yardstick: This is important for measuring lengths of fabric and for marking straight lines. Make sure that it is not warped, and that the markings appear on both sides.

Tailor's chalk: This comes in several colors, but white is easiest to remove. Keep the edge sharp. You also can use a dressmaker's pencil, which has a brush for removing the marks.

Pencil: For copying patterns onto tracing paper, a soft pencil, such as a 2B, is the easiest to use.

CUTTING

Pinking shears: The serrated blades make a zigzag cut. Use them to trim raw edges, especially on fabrics that fray easily.

Cutting scissors: These should have a 6-inch blade and be flat on one side. Never use on any other material except fabric.

Needlework scissors: Use these for snipping threads, cutting into or notching seams, and other close trimming jobs.

Paper scissors: Use them to cut paper templates and patterns, but never use them on fabric or thread.

STITCHING

Pins: Keep a range of sizes on hand. Those with glass or plastic heads are the most visible and easiest to use. Use a pin cushion to store pins when working.

Sewing needles: Keep an assortment of needles in your sewing kit. The most useful sizes range from three to 10. The higher the number, the finer the needle. Betweens are short, sharp needles that are ideal for fine hemming. Sharps, which are longer and allow more than one stitch on the needle at a time, are useful for basting or gathering. There also is a wide range of specialty needles available, including a tapestry needle, which has an eye large enough to take narrow ribbon.

Thimble: Use it to protect your fingertip when hand-sewing.

Threads: Mercerized cotton is ideal for stitching cotton or linen. Buy silk thread for silk fabric, cotton thread for wool, and a polyester/cotton mix for synthetic fabrics. Use a polyester thread for stretchy fabrics.

Needle threader: This tool has a flexible wire loop that you push through the needle's eye; insert thread into the loop, then pull the loop and thread back through the eye of the needle.

MACHINE WORK

Sewing machine: Essential for joining seams and hemming, a sewing machine makes quick work of home-sewing projects. A machine that does straight, zigzag, and reverse stitches is all you need to make the projects in this book.

Machine needles: Keep a range of sizes on hand. Choose fine needles and fine threads when working with fine fabrics; use thicker needles and thicker threads on heavier fabrics.

Machine feet: These come in a range of designs for specific jobs. Apart from a standard foot, you will find a one-sized zipper or piping foot, which can be adjusted to the right or left, a useful tool. A roller foot works well on shiny fabrics. A transparent foot, which allows you to see the fabric more easily, is helpful with appliqué work. Before you use a different foot on any sewing project, practice some stitching on a scrap piece of fabric to ensure satisfactory results.

Measuring and estimating

When you make your own bed covers, curtains, and bed linens, the first step is measuring to determine how much fabric you'll need. Use the instructions below to measure your bed, bed frame, and pillows, and refer to the individual projects to determine yardages accurately.

BED SKIRT

Measure the bare bed frame to estimate the fabric required for making a bed skirt. Whatever style of bed you have, the skirt needs to fall around the corners without interruption. Cut the base fabric roughly to size (this is called the platform). Lay this over the bed and draw around any posts and shaped corners, allowing ¾ inch for seam allowances. You may want to edge the platform with strips of the skirt fabric. The bed skirt can be made as a single unit or designed to split around corner posts. It also can be pleated or gathered along the length or at the corners. Measure the skirt, adding a 2½-inch hem allowance and ¾ inch to the top and sides. Allow 2½ times around the bed for gathers. The "pleats" at each corner are neater if made as separate flaps. Each flap should be 18 to 20 inches wide.

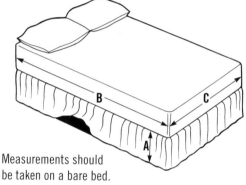

Measurements should
be taken on a bare bed.
A: Skirt length – top of base to floor
B: Mattress/base length
C: Mattress/base width

BED COVER

Take measurements over both summer and winter bedding to get the exact finished size. Generally you will need to allow an extra 1¼ inches on the bed height for summer bedding and 2 inches for winter.

A standard bed cover measures 80×100 inches. This makes a floor-length cover for a single bed or a skirt-length cover for a small 54×75-inch double bed.

A 100-inch square cover makes a floor-length cover for a standard 60×75-inch double bed and a top cover for a king-size 72×75-inch bed.

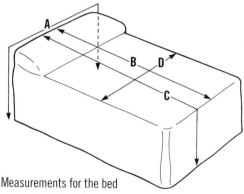

Measurements for the bed
cover should be taken over your usual bedding.
A: Twice the height of the bed over the pillows, plus the width
B: Top to the bottom of the bed
C: Top to the bottom, plus height at the bottom
D: Width of the bed

PILLOW

Pillows come in two shapes. The traditional pillow shape is a rectangle approximately 20×30 inches and the continental is a square, ranging from 26 to 30 inches square. Always measure your pillow forms before making the covers. When making covers, allow at least ⅝ inch extra in each direction, plus the seam allowances.

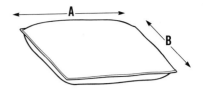

A: Length   B: Width

BED FRAME

Four-posters and half testers need one curtain to fit behind the headboard and either four bed curtains or two side curtains for the corners.

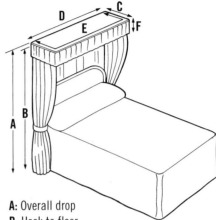

If you are refurbishing an existing frame, you will be able to use the original curtains as patterns. The amount of fullness you allow depends on the style of the bed. A substantial bed should have curtains that are heavy but not overly full. A light metal frame will take up to four times the fullness of fine fabrics.

If building your own frame, allow enough depth on the wood to include fittings for curtains, ceiling drape, and an outer valance. The frame should be approximately 6 inches larger all around than the bed to allow adequate space for bedding and curtains.

A: Overall drop
B: Hook to floor
C: Width of side curtains
D: Valance back curtain
E: Valance length, plus twice the width.
F: Valance drop

DUVET

Try to find wide-width fabric. However, if that is not possible and you want the duvet to match another fabric in the room, purchase a sheet for the underside and furnishing fabric for the top. Always leave the center fabric panel as a whole width of fabric with partial widths at each side. Then, cover the seams with an interesting tape, or accent them with piping.

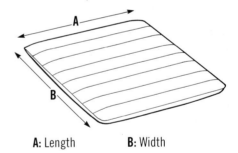

A: Length   B: Width

YOUR WORK SURFACE

A good work surface can save you a considerable amount of time and stress. Even if you are going to make just one item, it is worth spending a little time to prepare a good work surface. A dining room or kitchen table is adequate for smaller items, and the floor is fine for larger ones. The surface must be smooth, flat, and clean. It is helpful if you can leave your work spread out and undisturbed throughout the project.

For an "instant" worktable, cover a piece of sturdy fiberboard or plywood with an old blanket or curtain interlining, then cover it with a piece of canvas or curtain lining. Pull the fabric tight and staple it to the underside. Buy the biggest board that you can accommodate—a ¾-inch 4×8-foot board is ideal for most projects. Rest the board on a table, a guest bed, or on the floor. Store it in the garage for later use.

Seams

For a professional appearance and a long-lasting finish, make your stitching look as neat on the wrong side as it does on the right side. There are several ways to secure raw edges, and the choice of suitable techniques will depend on the weight and type of fabric used.

PRESSING SEAMS

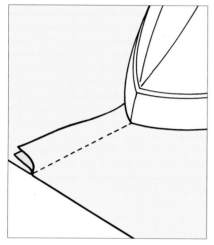

1 Press each seam as soon as you have sewn it. Work on the wrong side, following the line of stitches. Hold the iron over one area before lifting it and transferring it to the next.

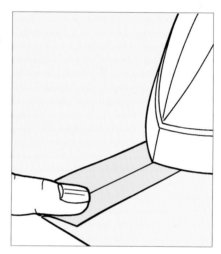

2 Slide your fingers down the seam to open it. Then use the point of the iron to press the allowance open. Then press the allowance on each side, using the full base of the iron.

PRESSING DELICATE FABRICS

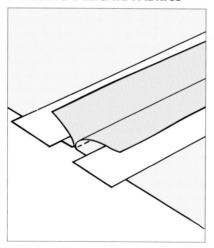

If pressing a seam may mark the fabric, cut strips of cardstock and slip them under the seam allowance to protect the fabric. Fabric with a deep pile, such as velvet, is easily crushed. With the velvet wrong side up and a spare piece of velvet underneath, pile side up, press the seam, using a steam iron and minimal pressure.

NEATENING SEAMS

To avoid raw edges fraying, it is best to neaten the edges of seam allowances. There are several ways to secure raw edges. The most suitable technique depends on the weight and type of fabric used.

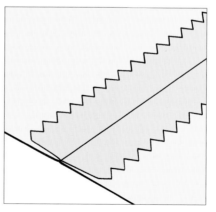

Pinking is a quick and easy method of finishing seams on cotton and fine fabrics that do not fray. Test on a fabric scrap before cutting the finished seam.

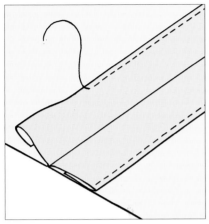

Straight-stitched folded edges are ideal for lightweight to medium-weight fabrics that are not bulky. Turn under each raw edge of the seam allowance ¼ inch; press, then straight-stitch the folded edge, keeping the main fabric free.

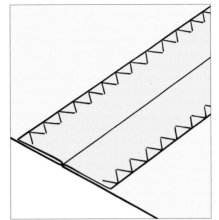

Zigzag edging is the most commonly used method for neatening raw edges and is good for bulky fabrics and those that fray. Stitch with a short, narrow zigzag, then trim just short of the stitches. On fabrics that fray easily, use a wider stitch.

FLAT-FELL SEAM

The raw edges of a flat-fell seam are encased within the seam line, but, unlike a French seam, both lines of stitching appear on the surface of the fabric.

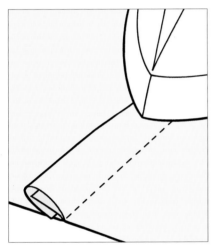

1 With right sides together, machine-stitch ⅝ inch inside the raw edges. Press the seam allowance to one side. Trim the underside of the seam allowance to ¼ inch.

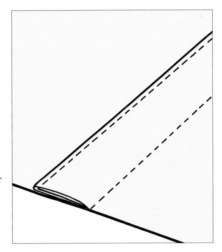

2 Press the wider seam allowance in half, encasing the narrower seam allowance. Press. Pin the seam flat on the fabric. Baste, then machine-stitch close to the folded edge.

FRENCH SEAM

This seam encloses the raw edges of fabric, and is used when an untidy edge might be visible. With the wrong sides of fabric together, stitch approximately ¼ inch from the raw edges. Refold with right sides together. Pin and stitch again just beyond the first stitching line, enclosing the raw edges within the seam. When stitching heavier fabrics, allow ⅜ inch for the first stitching line.

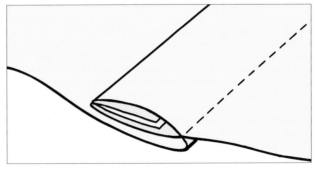

Hand stitches

Hand-sewing is necessary for specific stages of the assembly process and creates a professional-looking finish. The stitches illustrated here are used to make the projects in this book.

SLIP-STITCHING

Slip-stitching creates a neat finish for all hems, because the stitches are almost invisible on the right side of the fabric.

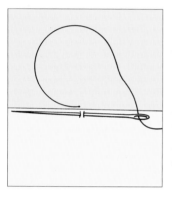

1 Fasten the thread with a backstitch within the hem, then bring the needle out on the folded edge of the hem. Pick up one or two threads from the main fabric, close to the hem.

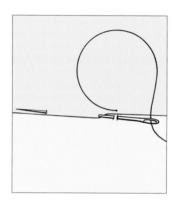

2 Take a ⅜- to ¾-inch-wide stitch along the fold of the hem and pull the thread through. Continue picking up threads from the main fabric and taking stitches along the hem edge until the hem is stitched.

LADDER STITCH

This is used to join two folded edges together and to close a gap left in the stitching when turning fabric through to the right side.

1 Fold under a narrow hem on both pieces of fabric to be joined. Baste loosely to hold the folded edges together. Make a small stitch to fasten the thread within the fold.

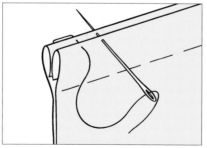

2 Bring the thread out on the outer side of one fold. Make a small stitch along the fold, then push the needle through the fabric on the opposite fold.

3 Continue until the opening is closed. Try to make the stitches and thread as invisible as possible, but do not pull the thread too tight. The stitches should be ½ inch in length.

LOCKSTITCH

Used to join two layers of fabric together so they act as one, lockstitch is worked vertically to join the seams and then once or twice more between the seams.

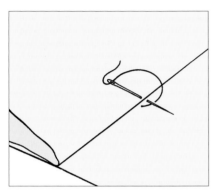

1 Lay fabric together with wrong sides facing. Pin on the center line, vertically down the length of the fabric. Fold back the lining to the pinned line.

Starting about 12 inches from the lower edge, secure the thread in the lining with a knot. Make a tiny stitch in the main fabric, picking up just one thread. Leave a 1-inch gap, then take a one-thread stitch from the lining back to the top fabric, working over the thread to form a simple loop.

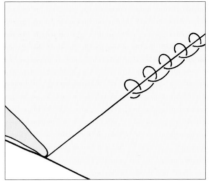

2 Continue making locking stitches every 1 inch until you reach the top edge. Keep the thread very loose so the fabric doesn't

pucker. Unfold the fabric before smoothing the layers back together. Make another vertical row of pins 15 inches from the last. Fold back the lining. Continue making rows of stitches across the complete width of the fabric until the layers are joined and can be handled as one.

PATTERN MATCHING

This is the professional method used to baste two pieces of patterned fabric together. Stitches are worked from the right side of the fabric, so you can make sure the pattern matches across the seam. It can be used as a permanent seam if you take smaller stitches.

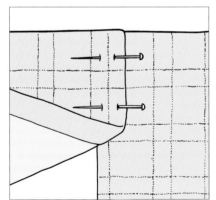

1 On one of the two pieces of fabric to be joined, press under ½ inch along the edge. Then place this folded edge, with raw edges matching, over the second piece of fabric. Match the pattern and pin in position.

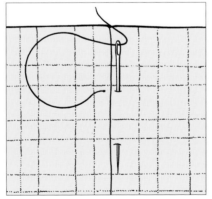

2 Secure the thread with small stitches within the fold line. Make a small stitch across to the flat fabric. Bring the needle out ½ to ¾ inch further down the seam line, running directly down the side of the fold.

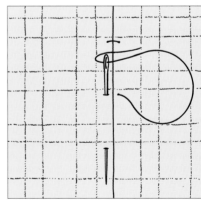

3 Take the needle straight across the fold and push it down inside the folded edge for another ½ to ¾ inch. Repeat these two stitches for the length of the seam. Turn the fabric to the wrong side to finish the seam.

FRENCH KNOT

These small surface knots are used to add detail to embroidered curtains and bedding.

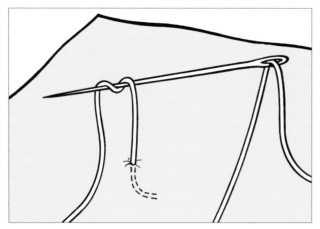

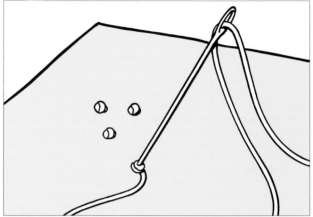

1 Push the needle up through the fabric where you want to make the first knot. Pull the thread taut with one hand while twisting the needle around the thread one or two times.

2 Push the needle back through the fabric at the point where it emerged, leaving a knot on the surface of the fabric. Fasten off the thread or go on to the next stitch.

SATIN STITCH

Satin stitch can be done on any swing needle sewing machine or by hand.

CROSS-STITCH

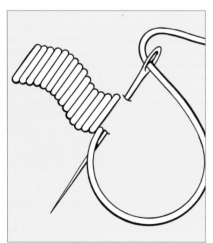

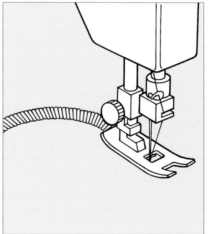

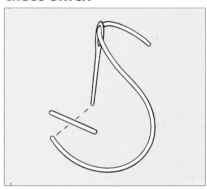

By hand: If the stitching area will not fit under your machine foot or if you prefer to embroider by hand, use a threaded embroidery needle and make long, straight stitches. Space the stitches close together, keeping the thread flat.

By machine: Set the zigzag button so the stitches are wide and close together. It may appear as a buttonhole stitch on your machine. Always test the stitch on a spare piece of fabric for length of stitch and spacing.

The simplicity of basic cross-stitch makes it highly popular. On soft furnishings, stitches usually are worked by making a row of even, slanted stitches across the fabric from right to left, laying down half the crosses; then work back from left to right to complete them. When the stitches are to be seen from both sides of the fabric, make sure the back of your work is as neat as the front.

GATHERING

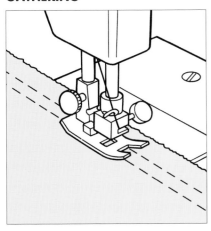

1 Set your machine to the setting for the longest straight stitch, and make two lines of stitching about ¼ inch apart. Work in 24-inch sections.

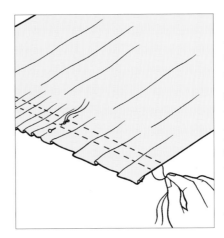

2 Pull up the two lines of threads, checking that the gathers are even along the fabric. Secure pulled threads around a pin until you're ready to assemble the project.

HERRINGBONE STITCH

This is the stitch used to fix a raw-edge hem in position prior to covering it with a lining, or to attach curtain interlining.

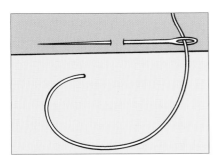

1 Baste the hem or interlining in place. Secure the thread with a few stitches, then bring the needle up through the hem, working from left to right. Take the thread diagonally into the main fabric and take a small backstitch, picking up one to two threads.

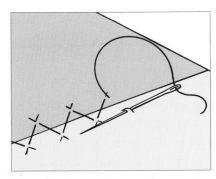

2 Still working diagonally, move across to the hem or interlining and make another small backstitch through the top layer only. Continue in this way, making stitches on both fabrics to the end of the seam before securing the thread.

BLANKET (BUTTONHOLE) STITCH

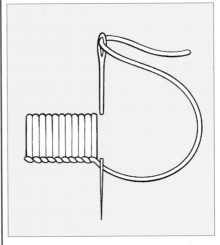

This stitch is used to make buttonholes or to strengthen an edge. Scroll-like stitches are worked close together, forming a firm edge that resists abrasion.

When the stitches are worked further apart, the embroidered edge is called blanket stitch. It is used to cover a raw edge or worked over a folded edge. Make the stitches of equal length and parallel to each other. Working from left to right, push the needle up through the fabric on the lower line, then insert it a short distance away on the upper line. Working back towards the lower line, bring the needle out close to where it first emerged, looping the thread under the needle. Pull up the thread to form a scroll-like base on the edge of the fabric. Continue making stitches in this manner all along the edge of the fabric or around the buttonhole.

Closures

Openings can be as unobtrusive as zippers or as showy and decorative as brightly colored buttons, ribbon loops, or ties. When the closure is also a decorative feature, it adds extra dimension to the finished design.

FOLDED TIES

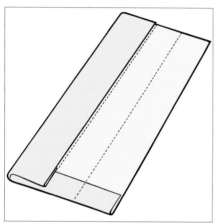

1 Cut a strip four times the width of the finished tie and 1⅛ inches longer. Turn under one short end ¼ inch, then press the strip in half lengthwise.

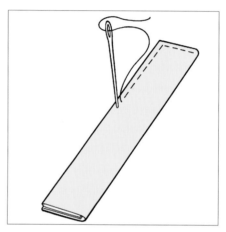

2 With wrong sides together, fold each side to the middle. Press. Fold over again, and stitch the short and long side together close to the folded edge.

ROULEAU TIES

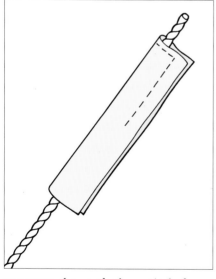

1 Cut a strip of fabric four times the width of your finished tie and 1⅛ inches longer. Fold in half lengthwise with right sides together, enclosing a length of cord. Stitch across one end to secure the cord, then stitch down the length close to the cord (about halfway across the fabric's width).

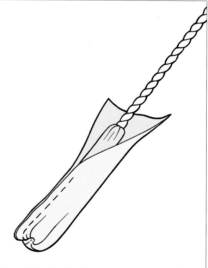

2 Trim back the fabric raw edges to ⅛ inch, then clip across the stitched corner to reduce the bulk. Pull the cord gently from the free end, at the same time turning the rouleau right side out. Cut the cord, fold the remaining raw edges to the inside, and slip-stitch closed.

PLACKET CLOSURE WITH TIES

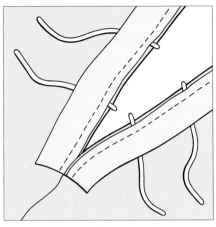

1 Cut two lengths of fabric, each 5 inches wide and 1⅝ inches longer than the opening. Mark the tie positions on both sides of the opening and pin in place. Pin one of the plackets to each side of the opening, with right sides together, over the ties.

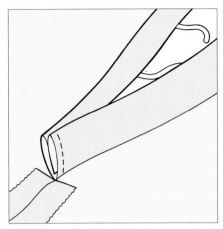

2 Stitch along the seam allowances. Press each strip into thirds, enclosing the raw edges. Using small stitches, slip-stitch along the length of both strips to hold them in place. Pin the short, raw ends of the plackets together. Stitch to hold in place.

PLACKET CLOSURE WITH BUTTONS AND ROULEAU

A rouleau of ribbon can be inserted into the placket to loop over each button. Gauge the ribbon length to suit the button size. The loops are attached to the right side of the fabric with the loop ends enclosed within the placket pieces.

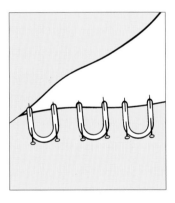

1 Cut two lengths of fabric, each 5 inches wide and 1⅝ inches longer than the opening. Mark the button positions. Cut short lengths of ribbon, then pin them in loops to one side of the opening.

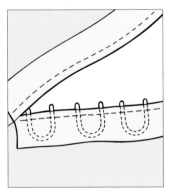

2 On the right side of the fabric and with right sides together, pin the placket strips down the sides of the opening, securing the rouleau loops to the fabric. Stitch along the seam allowance. Press.

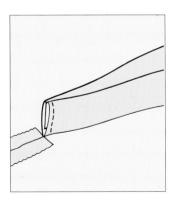

3 Fold each strip into thirds to enclose the raw edges. Slip-stitch along the length of both strips to hold them in place. Pin the short, raw edges of the placket strips together. Stitch to hold them in place.

4 Stitch a button to the placket edge to correspond to each rouleau loop. Press carefully on both sides, then slip the rouleau loops over the buttons to close the opening.

Piping

Piping fabric can be cut on the straight or cross grain of the fabric. If the piping is used in straight lines, it will be easier to handle if the fabric is cut on the straight grain. If it is to be curved around corners, it should be cut on the bias. To make piping, cut 1½-inch-wide strips of fabric. Cut slightly wider strips (about 2⅛ inches wide) for loose covers. To minimize bulk, all joins should be made on the diagonal, and the ends should be cut at 90-degree angles.

CUTTING THE PIPING FABRIC

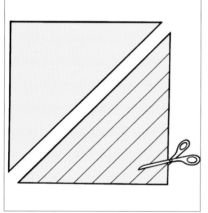

1 With the fabric flat on the table, fold one bottom corner up on the diagonal, making a triangle. Cut along the fold line. Mark pencil lines the width of the strip, following the cut line across the fabric. Cut along these lines. Repeat for the other triangle.

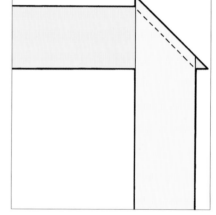

2 With right sides facing, hold two strips of fabric together as if making a continuous strip of piping. Turn the top strip over so that it is at a 45-degree angle to the first. With raw edges even, pin, baste, then stitch along the seam line.

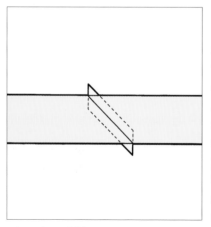

3 Join enough lengths of fabric until you have one continuous strip long enough to fit around the edge of the item you are making. Open out the seams, and trim away the extra triangles of fabric on the seam allowances. Press seams flat from the right side of the fabric.

MAKING THE PIPING

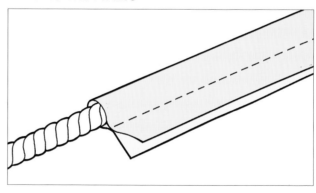

Fold the length of piping fabric in half lengthwise with wrong sides facing. Insert the piping cord. Machine-stitch along the length, encasing the cord.

JOINING PIPING

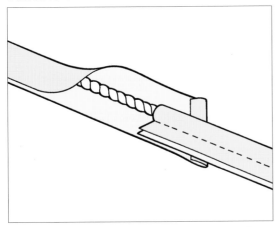

After the piping is attached and stitched nearly to the starting position, cut away the excess piping, leaving a 2⅜-inch overlap. Remove the casing stitches and cut away the cord so that the two ends butt together. Fold the casing fabric across at a 45-degree angle and cut along this fold. Turn under ⅜ inch, and pin securely before stitching along the remainder of the piped edge.

PIPED SEAMS

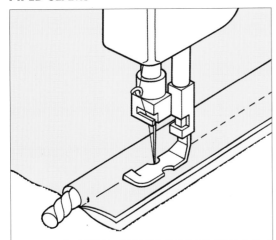

1 Always attach the piping so the raw edges of the piping align with the raw edges of the main fabric. The seam allowance is usually ⅝ inch wide. Pin along the stitching line and also at right angles, especially near the corners. To help keep the piping flat, these right-angled pins can be left in place while machine-stitching. Using a piping foot on the machine, stitch down the seam line.

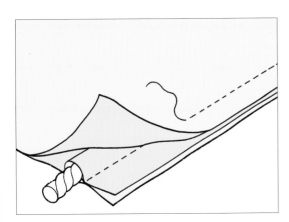

2 Place the second fabric piece over the first with right sides together, encasing the piping cord and matching the raw edges. Pin, baste, and stitch down the seam line again, using the previous stitching line as a guide.

CURVED SEAMS

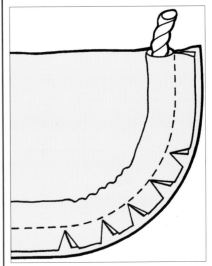

The piping cord should be snipped at ⅜- to ¾-inch intervals to stay flat around a convex curve. Notches will need to be cut away at similar intervals for a concave curve.

SHARP CORNERS

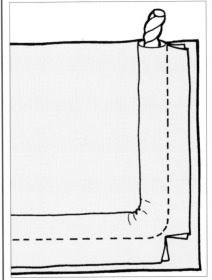

At each corner, stop ⅝ inch from the turn and snip to the piping stitching line. Fold the piping sharply and pin it in place to make a square corner.

Fabric care

After you've invested your time (and money) in stitching up custom-made furnishings, you'll want to keep them as attractive as possible. Regular cleaning and pressing will also extend the life of the fabrics.

EVERYDAY CARE

Along with accidental spills and staining, dust, cigarette smoke, and smoke from fireplaces are the main threats to soft furnishings. Regular vacuuming to remove particles of dust or smoke before they become embedded will help to extend the life of fabric. Furnishings should be vacuumed with a soft brush attachment. Vacuum with the grain of the fabric, not against it.

Be very careful with stain-removal products, because spot treatments can easily end up as permanent marks. It's best to choose washable fabrics for furnishings, especially if you'll be using them constantly.

Modern printed or dyed fabric resists fading well, although all fabric eventually will fade. Wherever possible, protect fabric from long exposure to direct sunlight, especially when only part of the fabric is exposed. Fading will show much more when it is next to an area protected from the sun. Lining helps protect curtains from fading, as does drawing them back during the day.

Make sure curtains and blinds do not hang too close to windows or radiators. Condensation and excessive heat—especially in combination—can cause fabrics to deteriorate.

WASHING AND CLEANING

Wash items before they become badly soiled, and treat stains immediately. When you buy fabric, check the manufacturer's recommendations for laundering and water temperature. To avoid shrinkage and fading, wash bed linens in warm, not hot, water.

If you are laundering ready-made items, check the manufacturer's instructions. The cleaning procedures are indicated by a standard set of symbols stitched into a seam line (these also can be found on clothing). When dry-cleaning is advised, there still may be some minimal shrinkage due to the process used. Some fabrics, such as chintz, need to be dry-cleaned in a non-water-charged system. Make sure your dry cleaner is knowledgeable. If shrinkage has occurred, it may be possible, in some cases, to iron the damp fabric in the direction of the shrinkage while gently stretching it. Always test the fabric for shrinkage before stitching bathroom furnishings.

If you are unsure if a fabric is colorfast, check it before washing it with other items. Dip a small, hidden area in warm water, then place this damp area between two white cloths and iron until the fabric is dry. If there is any color on the cloths, the fabric is not colorfast, and the item should be washed separately.

Never use bleach when washing soft furnishings. Most laundry detergents contain some bleaching or brightening enzymes. To prevent colors from fading, it may be advisable to use a mild liquid detergent.

DRYING AND PRESSING

Do not dry fabric too quickly, as this could result in shrinkage and creasing. This is especially important when tumble drying. When ironing, be sure to set the iron at the correct temperature. For best results, iron fabric while it is damp. Iron chintz on the right side with a dry iron (no steam).

To press embroidery, place the piece facedown over a soft towel to avoid flattening the stitching. Take care with rayon thread and any metallic or glittery yarns. The iron easily could melt your stitchery. Do not press lace. Lay it out flat, pin it in position, and then let it dry.

STAIN REMOVAL

- When removing a stain, never scrub it. This will simply spread the damage. Instead, work from the edges, dabbing at the stain until it disappears.

- On liquid stains, including wine, cover the area with salt to draw up as much liquid as possible. Then let the item soak in cold water for 30 to 60 minutes. Finish by washing in the usual manner.

- Tea and coffee stains should be soaked immediately in stain remover, then washed in the usual manner.

- On fruit and fruit-juice stains, rub fabric with salt before soaking in cold water. Rub with undiluted liquid detergent. Finish by washing in the usual manner.

- On biological stains, such as blood or milk, soak fabric in stain remover before washing.

- With solids, scrape off as much as you can with a flat knife before treating the stain.

WHAT CAN GO WRONG?

Shrinkage is the main problem caused by improper cleaning. All woven fabrics tend to shrink, especially those made of natural fibers, such as cotton. It is normal for furnishing fabrics to shrink about 5 percent when washed. Dry-cleaning also can cause shrinkage, but to a lesser degree. It is sensible to make curtains with a generous hem, and leave them loosely tacked in place until after the first laundering. Avoid bleaches of any sort, including laundering liquids and detergents with added bleach. Don't dry fabrics too quickly or with too much heat. Iron while damp and with the iron set at the right temperature. Above all, if you have the laundering instructions, follow them carefully.

CUSHION CARE

- Shake out and air pads regularly. Hang the cushions outside in a cotton bag on warm days to freshen the fabrics and feather filling.

- When washing covers, close zippers and fastenings.

- Wash feather forms in warm soapy water and rinse well. Keep shaking as they dry. Wash synthetic forms by hand or machine and tumble dry. Do not dry clean—the filling can absorb toxic cleaning-fluid fumes. Wash foam forms gently in warm, soapy water. Rinse, squeeze well, and dry in a warm place away from direct heat.

- Press covers while damp to iron out creases.

Glossary

Appliqué
A design created when one fabric or shape is applied to another.

Basting
A temporary stitch to hold fabrics in position and act as a guide for permanent stitching.

Batting
Bonded fabric, in various thicknesses, used to add depth and warmth to another fabric.

Bed skirts
Bed skirts fit over the frame of the bed and along one to four sides, depending on the style of the bed.

Bias
The diagonal line of fabric formed when the lengthwise grain of the fabric is folded to meet the crosswise grain of the fabric.

Bodkin
A large, flat needle with a blunt end and a large eye, used for threading ribbon, cord, and elastic through narrow channels.

Damask
Fabric woven with a pattern visible on both sides.

Double hem
When fabric is folded twice so that the raw edge is hidden within the hem.

Flat seam
Simplest way to join two pieces of fabric together. Fabrics are placed right sides together, machine-stitched along a seam line parallel to the fabric raw edge, and then pressed open.

Flat-fell seam
A very tough seam where the raw edge is encased within the seam and both lines of stitching appear on the surface.

French seam
A neat, narrow seam which is really two seams, one enclosed within the other. Ideal for use on sheer fabrics.

Gathering
A running or machine stitch that is pulled up to regulate the fullness of a piece of fabric.

Grain
The direction in which the fibers run in a length of fabric.

Interlining
An extra layer of fabric, placed between the main fabric and lining, to add insulation, thickness, and weight.

Ladder stitch
An almost invisible stitch used for securing hems or joining two folded edges on the right sides of the fabric.

Medium-density fiberboard
A composition board made of pressed wood fibers. It is very strong and will not splinter when cut. It comes in several thicknesses.

Miter
A corner seam that neatly joins two hems at right angles to each other.

Muslin
Strong, inexpensive woven cotton fabric, available unbleached or bleached.

Organdy
Fine, translucent cotton muslin, usually stiffened.

Organza
Thin, transparent silk or synthetic dress fabric.

Pattern matching
The professional method used to baste two pieces of a patterned fabric together so that the pattern matches across the seam.

Pattern repeat
The depth of one complete design in a length of fabric, which is then repeated along the cloth.

Pin tucks
A narrow stitched fold which provides a decorative feature.

Piping
A folded strip of fabric, inserted into a seam as an edging. It can be flat or form a covering for piping cord.

Placket
Fabric used to line an opening or slit for fastenings.

Preshrinking
Laundering fabric and trimmings before they have been made up. This prevents shrinkage when you launder the finished piece.

Quilting
The stitches used to decorate and hold two pieces of fabric in position, with padding between.

Seam allowance
The area between the seam line and the raw edge. The seam allowance needs to be trimmed, especially on fabric that frays easily.

Seam line
The line designated for stitching the seam.

Selvage
The nonfraying, tightly-woven edge running down both side edges of a length of fabric.

Toile de Jouy
A traditional French printed cotton that is perfect for bedrooms. The fabric falls and drapes well, is usually washable, and is always easy to handle.

Topstitch
A line of stitching on the right side of the fabric, often used as a decorative highlight.

Zigzag stitch
Machine stitch used to neaten seams. It also can be used as a decorative stitch.

Index

Meredith® Press
An imprint of Meredith® Books

Do-It-Yourself Decorating
Step-by-Step Bed and Bath Projects
Editor: Vicki L. Ingham
Technical Editor: Laura H. Collins
Contributing Designer: Jeff Harrison
Copy Chief: Angela K. Renkoski
Electronic Production Coordinator: Paula Forest
Editorial and Design Assistants: Barbara A. Suk, Jennifer Norris, Karen Schirm
Production Director: Douglas M. Johnston
Production Manager: Pam Kvitne
Assistant Prepress Manager: Marjorie J. Schenkelberg

Meredith® Books
Editor in Chief: James D. Blume
Design Director: Matt Strelecki
Managing Editor: Gregory H. Kayko
Executive Editor, Shelter Books: Denise L. Caringer

Director, Sales & Marketing, Retail: Michael A. Peterson
Director, Sales & Marketing, Special Markets: Rita McMullen
Director, Sales & Marketing, Home & Garden Center Channel: Ray Wolf
Director, Operations: Valerie Wiese
Vice President, General Manager: Jamie L. Martin

Meredith Publishing Group
President, Publishing Group: Christopher M. Little
Vice President, Consumer Marketing & Development: Hal Oringer
Meredith Corporation
Chairman and Chief Executive Officer: William T. Kerr
Chairman of the Executive Committee: E.T. Meredith III

Cover photograph: George Wright
First published 1998 by Haynes Publishing
Sparkford, Nr Yeovil, Somerset BA22 7JJ, UK

All of us at Meredith® Books are dedicated to providing you with information and ideas you need to enhance your home. We welcome your comments and suggestions about this book on Bed and Bath Projects. Write to us at: Meredith® Books, Do-It-Yourself Editorial Department, RW–206, 1716 Locust St., Des Moines, IA 50309–3023.